Defusing Angry People

Defusing Angry People

Practical Tools for Handling Bullying, Threats and Violence

By Kevin Fauteux, Ph.D., MSW, M.Div.

New Horizon Press
Far Hills, NJ

References:

American Psychological Association. "Controlling anger before it controls you." American Psychological Association. http://www.apa.org/topics/anger/control.aspx.

New Horizon Press
P.O. Box 669
Far Hills, NJ 07931

Fauteux, Kevin
Defusing Angry People: Practical Tools for Handling Bullying, Threats and Violence
Cover design: Robert Aulicino
Interior design: Susan M. Sanderson

Library of Congress Control Number: 2010928593

ISBN 13: 978-0-88282-349-2
New Horizon Press

Manufactured in the U.S.A.

15   14   13   12   11   2   3   4   5   6

AUTHOR'S NOTE

The information contained herein is offered for general education purposes only and is not meant to be a substitute for professional evaluation and therapy. Any of the treatments or methods described to manage or control anger should be discussed with a licensed health care/mental health practitioner. The author and publisher assume no responsibility for any adverse outcomes which derive from the use of any of these treatments in a program of self-care or under the care of a licensed practitioner. Any application of the recommendations set forth in this book is at the reader's discretion and sole risk.

This book is based on both first-person research and client interviews. In order to protect privacy, fictitious names and identities have been given to all individuals in this book and otherwise identifying characteristics have been altered. For the purpose of simplifying usage, the pronouns his/her and s/he are often used interchangeably.

CONTENTS

We have all encountered angry people and each of us has, at times, felt angry. But today, anger seems to have become a more pervasive and sometimes violent presence in our lives. The daily aggravations and annoyances that frustrate people seem to anger and even enrage them more frequently than ever before. Minor traffic accidents lead to physical altercations while serious incidents—teenagers attacking and sometimes killing teachers, parents assaulting one another at children's sporting events, high school students bullying other teenagers on the Internet resulting in suicide and enraged employees going ballistic—are growing in frequency.

Todd, a store clerk, asked me why after twenty years without incident he had unsatisfied customers threaten him three times in the past twelve months. Steven, a practicing psychotherapist for fifteen years, wanted to know why more clients were resorting to violence and told me of having to hide beneath his desk from a shotgun-wielding client. Jenny, a mother, questioned whether her son's recent tendency to erupt in rage over seemingly insignificant situations was typical of adolescence or if she should be concerned her son might be doing drugs. Roger, an acquaintance, wanted to know how he should respond to a mean boss. Sue, an emergency room nurse, related to me how she was accustomed to having to manage the occasional difficult patient, but lately she had been having too many days when she went home exhausted after incidences of being spat on and viciously cursed out. Karen, a friend, asked if she should leave her partner of ten years, because he was becoming more verbally abusive and she was afraid it might escalate into physical abuse. Kelly, a teacher, wondered why there were more bullies in her classrooms and what she could do about it.

Unfortunately, I do not have the answer as to why there seems to be more anger and violence in our society. One reason may be, according to the American Psychological Association, that our society views anger as negative and while people are taught how to handle other emotions, they are not taught how to deal with anger constructively. After twenty years of clinical work with hostile individuals and contentious couples, with backstabbing family members and dangerous felons, with "jonesing" addicts and aggressive co-workers, with bullies and normally peaceful people who inexplicably "go ballistic", I have insights and practical tools to offer you—the teacher, social worker, receptionist, therapist, store clerk, doctor, nurse, parent, spouse or partner—on how to manage people in your professional or personal life who become angry and sometimes violent.

Some years ago I noticed a client menacingly staring at his social worker and when I intervened, the client suddenly struck me. I was simply trying to calm the situation and was not prepared for his physical response. I could not have predicted it, just as a local soccer coach could not have known that one of his players' parents was going to punch him and just as the victims of violence at Columbine High School could not have anticipated the terrible moment that was to disrupt and, for some, shatter their lives. But if we cannot precisely predict occurrences of rage or violence then all the more reason we should be prepared as best we can to manage them when they happen.

Reflecting on the incident of the belligerent client who struck me fifteen years ago, I wish I had, at the time, possessed the de-escalation skills to have identified his anger signs and a potential assault and the tools to have intervened accordingly. In these pages I will present the insights and techniques I have developed over the past fifteen years to defuse an angry person, to calm an agitated client, to "talk down" someone who is hostile or threatening and, when all else fails, to defend oneself when experiencing acts of violence.

Tom was late for his doctor appointment and became frustrated when the receptionist, Bonnie, told him the physician was no longer available. When he explained that he relied on public transportation and it was not his fault that the city bus broke down, the receptionist said it was not her fault either, to which he replied that she was a bitch who did not care that he would be without his medication. Bonnie told Tom not to use offensive language, which resulted in his making a veiled threat of what happens when he does not take his medicine.

Tom's anger began as frustration when the doctor was not there. Frustration is probably the most prominent cause of arousing anger. We feel frustrated and angry when, like Tom, we are denied something or in some way feel disrespected. Clients or customers become angry, because one more person in their day is telling them what to do or not to do. They get enough demands and frustrations from their jobs and relationships and now someone else is telling them they cannot get what they need. Tom became angry when denied his medication and that anger escalated into hostility. Ultimately, as we shall see, Tom's anger turned into violence when the receptionist was seemingly insensitive to his needs.

If you have experienced firsthand the verbal and even physical abuse of a person's anger, you might raise an objection such as, "Sure, Tom was unable to get his medication, but it was because he was late and I know lots of people who miss appointments and do not become abusive or threatening." This is true. Why do people like Tom yell and become threatening when you are simply trying to do your job? Why does someone "snap" at you when you accidently bump him or her on a crowded street? What causes a normally calm acquaintance to become infuriated over a minor misunderstanding? Why does a person in a line start pushing when everyone else is patiently waiting?

Several critical factors can contribute to making people angry. According to a report from the American Psychological Association, internal and external events can cause anger while, in other cases, some people are just more "hotheaded" than others. In Tom's case, he was frustrated from living in poverty and felt humiliated having to go to a free health clinic. He also had a childhood history of being abused and over time learned that anger protected him against feeling hurt whenever someone disappointed him. Other people become angry, because they have a diminished capacity to tolerate frustration or to control impulses. They never developed social skills to cope adequately with life's annoyances or demands. Any kind of negative reaction or denial of their wants or needs is dealt with by using anger. The little problems we all encounter in our daily lives are approached by these types of people as personal affronts or insurmountable obstacles.

Some people have psychological impairments that make them more prone to being angry, such as being paranoid or possessing a narcissistic or sociopathic personality disorder. Genetics might play a role in how people express anger, reveals the American Psychological Association, as some children are born more irritable and easily angered. Others are simply difficult or naturally belligerent people who use anger to manipulate or intimidate.

Certain situations can also contribute to why or how people become angry. On any particular day, for example, any of us could feel tired or unwell and be more susceptible to irritability. Being in crowds makes some people anxious; others become cranky when they are hot; some women's fluctuating hormones make them periodically less patient than normal while some men's testosterone-driven competitiveness brings out the aggressive worst in them. Or maybe a seemingly innocuous encounter elicits an earlier traumatic experience that makes an "average Joe" suddenly become a terror.

So too, certain physiological conditions—e.g., low blood sugar or organic brain damage—can make some people easily agitated while others become uncontrollably hostile. And in all areas of public service we seem to be more frequently encountering drug and alcohol related rage, including manic "jonesing" and street drugs that either escalate belligerent behavior or inhibit normative aggressive restraints.

Life would be easier if our fellow employees, clients, family or acquaintances did not become angry with us. While this is true for us, it would not necessarily be good for them. For most people, anger is a healthy emotional response to feeling frustrated or hurt. It is a legitimate reaction to an injustice; an expression of self-preservation when they or a loved one are threatened; a way of emotionally standing up for oneself when ignored or abused.

There is a vast difference, however, between standing up for oneself in order to be heard and standing up in order to abuse or knock down another person. Standing up for oneself is an image used throughout this work to describe the expression of anger at a particular stage, such as standing up against being hurt or standing up in order to hurt someone. Anger is what one feels while standing up is the aggressive giving voice or action to it, whether it is yelling, cursing, venting, "getting in your face", bullying or physically striking someone.

Most of us think of aggression as being destructive or harmful, which it can be when it is verbally or physically abusive. However, according to the American Psychological Association, aggression is people's instinctive response to express anger. It is the behavioral component; the mobilization of one's energy to act on anger in order, at its early stage, to overcome the obstacles that made one feel victimized and, at later stages, to do the victimizing. This work examines the various stages of anger—beginning with more manageable expressions such as frustration and defensiveness and leading to more toxic expressions such as hostility, rage, threats and violence—and provides appropriate suggestions to defuse anger and to protect oneself from harm.

The best method for us to utilize in order to handle the anger of others is intervention techniques. Ask yourself what Bonnie, the receptionist, could have done to prevent Tom's anger escalating from frustration to hostility and ultimately violence? The latter became inevitable when Tom's anger elevated into its final stage. At that point Bonnie's only recourse was to protect herself. If, however, she had effectively intervened earlier, at the first onset of Tom's frustration or even later when he became hostile, she might have talked him down from his anger before it escalated into violence. Throughout this work we will return to Tom's anger—and to the manner in which Bonnie responded to it—to demonstrate how to effectively defuse anger at particular stages of expression and how the failure to do so escalates anger to a more intense and intractable next stage.

Suggesting Bonnie should have successfully de-escalated Tom's anger is easier than doing it. Anyone who works with the public or has tried to calm an agitated acquaintance knows how challenging it is to manage another person's anger. As a professional therapist, I thought I excelled at defusing angry people, yet I missed vital signs when I was assaulted fifteen years ago. I still had much to learn about angry and violent people and what would have prevented that situation.

In trying to successfully cope with other people's anger, we all need to learn that a major reason a person's anger either escalates into violence or is defused is the manner in which we have previously tried to intervene in that particular situation. This does not mean you were responsible for the person's anger or that you should accept it. Bonnie should not be held accountable for Tom's frustration nor should she have to put up with his verbal abuse. But we are responsible for how we respond to a person's yelling, threats or cursing. How we respond will determine whether we contribute to the anger's de-escalation—to containing the rage or reining in the hostility—or we escalate it and inadvertently propel the emotion toward potential violence.

We will look at our own responses to anger. How you respond to someone's anger is determined first by your ability to accurately identify the nature of the anger. Two people can become incensed over the same situation in two entirely different ways. You tell one you are sorry you cannot help with the problem and he becomes frustrated; you say the same thing to the other and he becomes belligerent or threatening.

Stages of Anger

One day, I was in an extremely long line at the airport where I observed how differently people expressed their anger when told their flight was delayed. I saw all of the stages of anger, which we shall examine in this book:

1. Some people complained because they were *frustrated* waiting in line.
2. You could hear in the incensed voices of others a deeper and *defensive* response to feeling disrespected for being made to wait.
3. A man's argument with airline staff was clearly compelled by a need to demonstrate he was not going to accept their explanation without first being *difficult* about it.
4. A *hostile* woman tried to bully a staff member to let her proceed to the front, because she was in a hurry.
5. An *enraged* person ranted about how intolerable the situation was.
6. A man *threatened* an attendant with "You won't like what you see if you don't immediately help me!"
7. A person *violently* pushed an airline agent who would not let her pass.

How would you deal with any of these people if you were one of the airline staff members confronted with the customers' anger? Would you know the best way to defuse one person's yelling would be simply to listen while another person would need to be firmly told to stop yelling, and would you be able to identify which person's anger is which and why? Would you recognize whether a particular person's anger was a form of standing up for oneself in order to be assertive or a means to stand over others so as to aggressively push them around?

It would be easy—and potentially dangerous—to misinterpret a person's anger for early stage frustration when it is really later stage hostility—or vice-versa—and as a result intervene in a way that does not defuse the anger, but instead escalates it. One person's yelling might simply be a "bark worse than her bite" situation, meaning her anger is verbally but not physically abusive. It might even be a healthy, albeit loud, expression of standing up for herself and nothing more. If you misinterpret that anger to be later stage hostility or rage and respond by ordering her to stop yelling—when instead what she simply needs is to be heard—the person will feel at minimum misunderstood and possibly even threatened by your overreaction. Perhaps she will yell louder to get you to listen and you will become defensive to get her to stop shouting. This might continue until her anger eventually escalates from its original annoying "bark" to become the "bite" that your intervention inadvertently agitated. Instead you need to be able to recognize when a person's cursing or "getting in your face" is only a bark, an expression of frustration or a means of standing up for oneself. To do so allows you the enviable ability to intervene at this early stage when anger is still manageable, before it mixes with enough anxiety and hostility that it becomes unmanageable and explosive.

Also you want to recognize when anger is not about assertiveness and instead is manipulative or intimidating. If you try to help an intimidating or assertive person deal with his anger—to "get in touch with his feelings" or to vent his frustration, as you might do at an earlier stage of this person's anger—you would be mistaking the aggressive bark of his anger for mere frustration when instead it is a prelude to a pernicious bite.

Remember Tom who eventually physically attacked Bonnie for not giving him his medicine. Had Bonnie known how to recognize the difference between frustration and hostility and how to intervene accordingly—as too with me and my assaultive client—she could have intervened more successfully to defuse Tom's anger and save herself from harm. Bonnie and I should have been able to recognize in the angry people's behavior or words the indicators that their barks were more than simply venting anger and instead were clear warnings of the bites to come. Bonnie should have possessed the insights to recognize the depths of Tom's anger and the skills to defuse it while it was manageable. I, rather than thinking it was a frustrated client who could be calmed with good communication skills, should not have been surprised when he turned to hit me and instead should have anticipated the imminent danger and known how to protect myself.

Maybe you are not in a work environment where you are confronted by angry or potentially violent people. Instead think of another everyday type of encounter you might have had with an irate individual. Maybe it was with a spouse who snapped at you after a particularly difficult day at the office, an annoyed acquaintance or a bully at school. Consider the experience most of us have had being in a crowded room and accidentally bumping into a person who yells at you for spilling his drink. What do you make of his anger and how do you respond to it? Is it simply an instinctual reaction to being bumped or frustration for losing his drink; why is he still upset after you apologize and what more can you do to allay his anger; what if he calls you an idiot or bitch or accuses you of bumping him intentionally; should you be worried when he says you better buy him a new drink?

We will examine anger and de-escalation techniques that will help you "say the right thing" to defuse the incensed man angry over your accidental bump and would have helped both Bonnie de-escalate Tom's threat and me from being assaulted years ago. Fortunately, most of us will never be physically threatened, but we will have encounters with people who become angry because we accidentally bump them or because we are not able to give them what they want or for any number of reasons. We hope we have the "right thing to say" to stop their anger. Or, we think we know the "right thing to say" but saying it only makes them more upset. While no precise formula exists to perfectly defuse an irate person, the information in this book will, I hope, give you insights into people's anger and the techniques—the "right thing to say"—to intervene effectively and safely. It will aid in your recognizing the difference between a threat and the deed, between anger as an expression of frustration or bullying or that which is imminently violent. Here are the tips, techniques and strategies to defuse the bark and protect yourself against anger's bite.

CHAPTER 1

Knowing Yourself:
The First Tool of De-Escalation

First we need to examine how the angry person reaches in to you and how his or her yelling, demeaning language, hostility or threats affect you. This is important, because how his verbal abuse or temper tantrum affects you and how you manage its affect on you directly determine how you will defuse or possibly escalate that person's anger.

Even before we turn to the triggers of a particular situation we need to examine generally our own inner reactions when someone yells or "gets in your face." Knowing yourself and how you respond to anger—both your own as well as others'—is as important a tool in de-escalation as practical techniques such as "talking down" an enraged person. Knowing yourself means understanding your instinctual response to being yelled at or intimidated as well as your emotional and cognitive response, which we will examine later in this chapter.

What is the first thing that occurs when someone curses or bullies you? Most of us say we think of the best way to calm the person. Actually our first response is not to think about what to do, but instead is to feel something. We feel frightened when threatened;

anxious when an enraged person appears out of control; disrespected when cursed at; stressed when having to cope with someone's yelling; intimidated when someone "gets in your face." Our minds take this information and collaborate with our bodies to shift into a self-protective *fight/flight* mode.

Fight/flight is the instinctual response to feeling verbally abused or physically endangered that protects us from harm. What happens is that being cursed or bullied stimulates our brains to activate neurotransmitters that set off chain reactions of protective measures in the sympathetic nervous system. Foremost among these is the production of adrenaline, which contributes to self-preservation instincts. It does this by getting more blood pumped to muscles for greater strength, stimulating the liver to produce more sugar for an immediate influx of energy and increasing respiration so as to enrich the blood with more oxygen, among other things. These physiological functions give you the stamina to manage the person who yells at you and an extra boost to refuse to be intimidated by the person who "gets in your face." Your instinctual response to feeling in harm's way is your body's way of saying, "I'm not taking this lying down."

The problem with our body's fight/flight response is that while it is great for protecting us from irate and hostile people, it is not so good for de-escalating another person's anger. Instead it can make the angry person even louder or more belligerent. The adrenaline-fortified blood gives us the energy to defend ourselves against physical or verbal abuse, but also causes us to approach a person's anger out of confrontation rather than resolution. It turns our intervention into a contest in which we must win and the angry person must lose. As we will examine throughout these pages, we generally approach irate people trying to subdue or silence their anger rather than understand and help them more maturely manage it. We stifle a person's shouting when we should be listening to why she is yelling. We imperiously declare, "No one talks to me that way" instead of "talking down" the verbally abusive person. Similarly we "get in the face" of the individual who is fiercely "in your face" rather than giving the physical/emotional space needed to make him comfortable enough to "save face." In those fortunately rare moments that most of us will never have to know when we are actually confronted by an assailant with a weapon, we try to grab the weapon rather than take a moment to more clearly assess our options to protect ourselves. Each of these interventions does not defuse anger and instead escalates it.

Let me be unequivocally clear: you should not have to accept someone's demeaning language and should always defend yourself against harm. That is not the problem with our responses to people's anger. The problem is not *that* we protect ourselves against verbal or physical abuse, but *how* we protect ourselves. You may learn all the de-escalation tools this work offers, but it will have little effect if your reaction to the angry person causes him to be defensive rather than responsive to your intervention. You will be required in certain circumstances to more firmly demand that someone stop yelling or "back off." What determines those circumstances will be a salient discussion of this work. But too many times I have observed people, like those previously discussed, whose orders to a volatile individual to stop yelling caused that person to yell louder, because she was only yelling in the first place to be heard and an order for her to stop yelling obviously meant she was not being heard; whose declaration, "You can't talk to me that way" did not result in an "okay" and instead instigated a hostile, "What are you going to do about it"; whose response, "Get out of my face" caused a person to get more physically "in her face"; whose attempt to snatch a person's weapon resulted in physical injury.

All of these responses to angry people make them angrier; they do not help de-escalate the anger. These interventions are in part the product of a person's instinctual reaction to being yelled at or bullied. The first step in responding to a person's anger is not to react and instead to stay calm.

Calm Yourself

One night after work I was thinking about a client whose particularly abrasive yelling earlier that day had "pushed my buttons" and resulted in my adamant demand that he stop yelling, which caused him to shout more forcefully. I was thinking about this interaction while surfing—where I do some of my best thinking as I wait for the next wave—when suddenly a huge wave came crashing toward me. How I reacted to that scary wave struck me as a good metaphor for how I had responded to that client and how we in general react to irate people. An aggressive side of me dictated that I should directly take on the wave in spite of the fact it was too big to ride. An anxious part of me instinctually wanted to paddle away from that wave even though it probably would have caught and pummeled me. And something inside me seemed to surrender any hope and freeze like a deer frightened in a headlight. But there was also a part of me that said to stay cool, to resist the impulse to flee or confront and thereby allowed a relatively calm moment in which to examine the wave and make an informed decision how best to deal with it. My angry client was like that big wave and the first step to managing either one is to refrain from overreacting by staying calm.

Staying calm when a person is screaming or threatening—as when a huge wave is about to crash on you—is easier said than done. We truly like to think we can always respond with equanimity, but a yelling or bullying person instinctually shifts us into the defensive fight/flight mode that compels us to react and confront rather than be calm and responsive. The latter is difficult when the activated adrenaline we discussed earlier is arousing us and our muscles are aching for action. You will have trouble remaining detached and taking the time to assess the situation when rapid breathing oxygenates blood and your liver pumps extra sugar into your blood so as to energize you to act *now*. All of this comes into play when an angry person makes you feel a little frightened and you want to stay calm but instead react defensively; when someone is aggressively "in your face" and you know you should try to "talk him down" but his intensity makes you anxious and something inside you wants to demand, "Get out of my face!"; when a person calls you a "bitch" or a "spick" and, in spite of knowing from this book that you should not let gender and racial epithets get to you, you feel the need to "put him in his place." All of these responses would escalate rather than defuse these peoples' anger.

Police departments throughout the country recognized within their own ranks this tendency to overreact to irate people (especially after the Rodney King incident in Los Angeles) and so began training their officers how to calm themselves when faced with an angry or threatening person. Escalating anger led police officers to beat and seriously harm Rodney King during an otherwise routine traffic stop. When a state court acquitted the officers of the beating, riots broke out throughout Los Angeles. Eventually, a federal court sent two of the four officers to prison. Leaders of police departments know police men and women can respond defensively to being disrespected or intimidated and so do not always respond calmly to an incensed person. Even after police officers control the situation—as when they had restrained Rodney King—they do not automatically calm down from their heightened physical responses and instead sometimes continue acting aggressively on their adrenaline.

No police department wants its officers to be bereft of this instinctual response that defends them from harm. A police officer—or teacher, social worker, store clerk, parent or partner—who is verbally or physically abused wants her body to quickly mobilize the energy to protect herself. I was grateful of this instinctual bodily response when I was hiking in Alaska and came upon a bear. My body immediately surged with the energy enabling me to run. It was the same with a co-worker who "knew in his gut" he should grab the gun of a client before he was shot.

It is good that your body quickly sets in motion the defenses to protect you from abuse—or is it? While it seems natural to "run for your life" if in the presence of a bear, many experts suggest you resist that impulse and try to appear non-aggressive. Unfortunately, the co-worker who grabbed the client's gun was shot. The fight/flight response neither defused these situations nor protected the people involved as it is wired to do. Instead it counterproductively escalated the volatility and increased the likelihood for violence.

Consider a less extreme example of Bonnie, the earlier mentioned receptionist who ordered the doctor's client, Tom, to stop yelling about not getting his medicine. She felt he had no right to talk to her the way he did—she was simply doing her job when she told him the doctor was no longer available because Tom was late—and she made it clear she would take no more. "You can't talk to me that way—it's not my fault you were late!" She of course was right that she should not have to accept being insulted, but the way she defensively reacted to Tom did not defuse his anger and instead escalated Tom's anger into increasingly more intense stages. Bonnie became anxious in response to his elevated anger and, combined with her own anger about having "had enough" of his abuse, she more aggressively demanded that he immediately stop his verbal mistreatment of her. This again did not defuse his anger and instead inflated it into becoming vicious: "Who are you to blame me, bitch; you don't know a thing about me!" This scared Bonnie and so she threatened to call the police, which resulted in Tom's daring her to call "and see what happens to you!" When she reached for the phone Tom struck her and fled. The physical violence climaxed an escalation of anger that began simply with Tom's frustration that he could not get his needed medicine and that was exacerbated at each anger stage by Bonnie's reaction to Tom's anger rather than a calm and reasoned interaction that would have defused it.

Good luck *not* responding defensively to someone's verbal abuse when protective instincts immediately arise and you hear that inner voice telling you, *How dare she call me that!* It is like telling yourself not to run from a charging bear or not to grab the gun that is pointed at you when impulses quicken and every muscle in your body is set in motion.

Staying calm and not yelling back at the angry person or not grabbing that gun might seem counterintuitive but it is what you need to do. You have to be able to resist the adrenaline driven impulse to react to a person's anger and instead stay calm. Resisting the impulse is not rejecting it nor is staying calm being passive (as we will examine shortly). It simply means you do not *have* to act on your visceral response to a person's verbal abuse—as if primitively controlled by an instinct to immediately stifle someone's shouting—and instead you have the equanimity to assess how aggressively or empathically you should respond. Staying calm creates a moment between impulse and acting on impulse in which you can decide if it is best to "listen to your gut" and run from the bear or roll into a self-protective ball; to grab the gun or try to "talk the person down"; to understand where the angry person is "coming from" or demand "Stop yelling now!"

Parasympathetic Nervous System

If you pause and stay calm rather than impulsively grab the gun or yell back at an angry person, the question remains: how do you do so when your instincts are compelling you to grab that gun or when the urge to yell back at the hostile person is irresistible? Part of the answer is found in the same internal physiology that not only makes us adrenaline driven, but also innately relaxes that hyper-defensive response. Your body cannot tolerate for too long the earlier described infusion of adrenaline that comes from the fight/flight response to feeling verbally or physically abused and prevents an overload via the parasympathetic nervous system which kicks in to lower your heightened blood pressure and slow rapid breathing. It helps you organically become calm.

However, it takes time for your body to relax from its heightened defensive state and you might not have time when an angry person is "in your face" and your body is tense with the energy that wants to react against—rather than listen to and understand—the angry person. You help your body relax by consciously making the effort to stay calm, which not only maintains your emotional equilibrium but, in effect, prods the parasympathetic function to temper the internal pressure to act impulsively.

For example, when a person threatens you by brandishing a weapon and you notice yourself breathing quickly or licking your dry lips (due to adrenaline's effect), tell yourself to breathe deeply or to slow down your breath. This will not only help you emotionally stay calm, but will also lower your accelerated heart rate and restore a normative amount of oxygen to your blood, thereby reducing fight/flight hyper-stimulated energy. As a result you will be less compelled to act recklessly, like attempting to grab an assailant's gun or defiantly demanding an angry person stop calling you names.

Maybe you feel your body tensing in response to a person yelling at you, a tension induced by the instinctual infusion of adrenaline into your blood and muscles. Instead of acting on that tension by yelling back at the person, you can, first, be attentive to where you feel tense. Watch for rigidity in your face (clenched jaw) and shoulder muscles. You can relax these muscles through techniques such as tightening and releasing them or simply telling yourself to relax them. You might notice yourself pacing due to the extra energy in your blood. Tell yourself to slow down. This counteracts the muscle's pressure to "pounce" on the angry person rather than reason with her.

You also have at your disposal the classic "count to ten" before you act, which is ideal for giving yourself moments in which to pause and stay composed before responding to an irate person. You can also use various visualization tools to help keep calm when you feel yourself becoming agitated or defensive: picture yourself staying "cool," for example, when your face feels flush or your body feels hot and your hands sweaty (due to increased blood flowing through your veins and your body cooling itself by stimulating sweat glands).

Besides relaxation techniques, slow your actual interaction with the angry person. If you notice you are talking to a hostile person faster or louder then usual, tell yourself to lower your voice and you will discover a lowering both in your heightened defensive reaction and in the tension of your interaction. It will also have the added effect of reassuring the irate individual that you are effectively handling her anger, thereby making her less agitated simply knowing someone is neither overwhelmed by it nor letting it spin out of control. It also models to the person how to stay calm when dealing with frustration and anger. You demonstrate in your voice as well as in your general body language (e.g., posture, gestures and facial expressions) how to deal with anger in a controlled rather than aggressive manner.

A final relaxation technique is simply telling yourself to stay calm. You have been bullied or insulted and you find yourself about to criticize or command respect. You know that reacting in this manner will only make the situation worse, so you actually say to yourself "I can handle this," "Take it easy" or "She's just angry; it's not personal." It is not easy to resist the instinctual "I'm not going to take it anymore!" Remind yourself it will only escalate the situation. Also remind yourself that if a person's aggressive body language or confrontational attitude can make you react in this defensive manner then so too the same adrenaline-induced effect can take place in that person when she sees it in you: all the more reason to be aware of how you respond to the irate individual and the importance of keeping calm.

These various techniques of recognizing and managing your internal response to an angry person are temporary solutions. They do not rid the yelling or bullying but instead help you stay in control so you can do what is necessary to defuse the anger. These techniques allow you to be reflective rather than reactive, to think before saying something that escalates rather than defuses anger. It is not important what technique you use, only that you have something that helps calm you when you recognize any of the signs of a tense reaction to an incensed individual.

Calm is Not Doing Nothing

Staying calm in response to the angry person is not the same as doing nothing. It is not a magical mental state entered by "tuning out" an incensed individual and "tuning in" your inner peacefulness. This ersatz calmness is frequently the domain of people who refrain from overreacting to conflict *not* as a way to defuse it and instead out of a need to avoid it. They generally are not comfortable with others' anger or with their own and may have difficulty saying "no" to someone's aggressive demands. So they "stay cool" and think if they avoid the conflict long enough it will correct itself or the angry person will eventually give up and go away. Or, they rationalize their reluctance to intervene as "not rocking the boat." They also might ignore a person's unacceptable aggressive behavior by dismissing it as inconsequential: "It's nothing—she's just blowing off steam." Or they say the angry person is under a lot of pressure and so needs to be given "some space" when the volatile situation actually requires immediate intervention with failure to do so resulting in a higher risk of escalated anger and possible violence. The propensity for the latter is even greater when, due to these people denying the severity of the situation, they are not prepared to manage it when it happens.

I have witnessed workers simply do nothing about a person's verbal abuse, because they think "it's part of the job" to be yelled at sometimes. Perhaps they are afraid others think this way and so are reluctant to validate the seriousness of a situation for fear others will consider them either overreacting or unable to handle it. Often I have observed people—especially those working in health care and social services—who only see good qualities in the people they help and so ignore their verbal abusiveness: "He is such a nice guy; he certainly couldn't be *that* angry."

To do nothing when someone is yelling is to invite more, not less yelling. The person will scream louder because, at minimum, he will interpret your doing nothing as not hearing the urgency of his anger. It is equally likely that he might see your passive response—your tentativeness, wishy-washy ways as well as possible physical manifestations such as a lowered head, averted eye contact and slouched posture—as an unwillingness to get involved or an inability to do anything about his yelling. Your reluctance to address his anger or even recognize it tells him you are unprepared to deal with it and makes him think you are either no help or even a hindrance to resolving what angers him. Maybe he sees in your calmness a front for fear, an indecisiveness born of being afraid to act (thus adding a third "F" to the fight/flight response: that of freezing). He perceives in your passivity a vulnerability that makes you someone easily intimidated or a doormat to be "walked all over."

Further, to do nothing about a person's anger can make him think he has been given license to act on his feelings. Once, I witnessed Carol, an agitated employee, tell a fellow worker, Bob, she was so angry she felt like breaking the lamp next to her. Bob commendably stayed calm and reassuringly said, "I can see you are so angry you want to break the lamp." But Bob never told Carol not to break it—either in a confrontational manner or by establishing strict limits to her threat, as we will examine later. The result was Carol—who desperately needed help controlling her impulses—did not feel any external constraints, so she broke the lamp. Or maybe Carol broke the lamp not because she had impulse control problems but because Bob's apparent disregard for her incensed exclamation made her feel she had been given implicit permission to do so.

I watched Frank become livid when Heidi, his social worker, did not give him the voucher he needed and, in a similar situation, I observed a customer explode in rage when the store clerk, Charlie, would not give him the refund he expected. Both workers did not respond aggressively to their respective customers' complaints, which was good. After being bombarded with more complaints and finally "having had enough" of their verbal abuse, both employees relented and gave each of the incensed persons what was demanded out of concern that to do otherwise would escalate the situation. The employees might have been correct in their assessments of intensifying anger, but their unwillingness to become involved in trying to contain the volatile situation told these people—and others witnessing their outbursts—that outbursts get what you want and temper tantrums will be indulged if you yell loud and long enough. I watched one of these people then boast to others how he got his way, further legitimizing anger as a tool that gets results.

Being passive not only avoids having to do something about a person's anger but also can be a subverted way of indulging one's own aggressive instincts and even indirectly inflicting them on the angry person. This is called passive/aggressive behavior. It is doing nothing as an aggressive act.

For instance, take a situation where a person yells at you and you don't speak, under the guise you are staying calm and not letting her get to you. Yet, in fact, you are not saying anything as a means of getting back at the person for yelling at you: it annoys her that you are calm instead of reacting. Or maybe you say, "I will sit here and wait for you to stop yelling at me," which further aggravates the person whose yelling was meant to get you to do something and thereby indirectly gratifies your aggressive wish to retaliate for the disrespect you had to endure.

A similar passive/aggressive response is to walk away from an irate individual or hang up the phone on someone who is verbally abusive, under the pretext of not "getting into the mix." While this might seem commendable for not escalating the situation, it more likely is a way of getting back at the person for disrespecting you, which you know is true when the person becomes angrier for it. (Walking away is not passive/aggressive in a violent situation when it is the only way to protect yourself, which we will examine in the section on violence.)

Being calm is neither passive nor passive/aggressive. Instead it allows an assertive response to an angry person. Assertiveness, as we shall see throughout these pages, is very different from an aggressive intervention with an incensed person. It reins in someone's hostility without being domineering; tells an irate individual not to yell and at the same time lets her know you are actively listening; and is being in control of a volatile situation but not being controlling. All of this helps defuse people's anger, because it respects them without indulging their inappropriate behavior and at the same time respects your own self-preservation instinct without indulging its impulse to aggressively overact to someone's yelling or bullying.

Counter-Transference and Anger

Staying calm helps you not overreact to an angry person, but frequently it is not their attitude or aggression to which you are overreacting. What makes you anxious or defensive is the misinterpretation of the person's anger due to the needs or fears it elicits within you.

Counter-transference is the term applied to feelings or needs we normally are not aware of, but that are triggered within us when encountering an angry person: feelings or needs which subsequently influence how we perceive and respond to that person. Maybe, for example, you were raised in a family that was uncomfortable with anger and you learned to deny it. You have a tendency to ignore it in others, because it brings up undesirable feelings in yourself, which you do not know how to manage. While you may have learned never to raise your voice or be aggressive, others, however, learned anger was an appropriate way of expressing themselves and sometimes the only way to be heard. You may feel uncomfortable when a person yells, even when it is only to get you to listen, and so rather than defuse the person's anger by listening you escalate it by minimizing or ignoring it.

I knew a loving husband named Peter who never responded to his wife Ashley's anger because to do so made him anxious, especially since he was never able to resolve her anger. This made Peter angry and was something he hated about himself. Ashley, however, was a very passionate person and anger came to her easily, so she interpreted Peter's reticence to respond to her passionate feelings either as ignoring her or as passive/aggressive behavior. This was a couple in need of counseling so as to learn to understand each other's way of expressing themselves, especially their anger.

You might have been raised thinking anger was an undisciplined emotion or that it demonstrated an immature lack of control. In this case you may feel a person's yelling is a childish temper tantrum and rather than taking the time to understand why she is angry, you sternly tell her, "Get a hold of yourself." Or maybe a person brusquely demands something from you and you get into an argument, because you have underlying issues around people who feel entitled. That is a personal weakness of mine. I want to snap back at the person who snaps his fingers and takes for granted that I am supposed to do something for him. Although it might be true that the person is an annoying narcissist, it is also true that my impatience with his sense of entitlement is what will produce a response from me that will escalate, not defuse his anger.

Maybe you take offense at a person cursing you, because it elicits from deep inside you an anxious equation that anger equals disrespect. You expect compliance with your request to stop shouting and, when it is not forthcoming, you feel belittled or your authority disrespected. What should have been a voice inside your head saying *I don't like being talked to that way* instead is replaced with *I'm not going to let her get away with talking to me like that!* You externalize this inner voice when you demand, "Stop talking to me that way!" You probably are not even aware of the aggressive tone of your voice, nor would you countenance the possibility that your response comes from an inner feeling of being offended by the person's anger. Instead you believe your response simply "sets the person straight" about what is acceptable and unacceptable behavior. You believe this even when your intervention does not result in defusing the person's anger and instead in her more aggressively saying it is you who should be set straight.

When everyone else perceives a particular person's yelling as simply venting frustration or responding to an injustice but you take it as a personal affront (and react accordingly), it is possibly because your own underlying feelings or needs spin it into something personal. And even when the anger *is* personal, the fear or anxiety it elicits can become entangled in your reaction and infuse it with an intensity inappropriate to what is needed to defuse the anger.

I have witnessed too many people attempt to defuse irate individuals only to exacerbate their anger due to the negative impact of that anger having had "pushed their buttons" and causing them to overreact. You can learn the many tools to de-escalate the incensed person, but if inner needs or preconditioned notions cause your intervention to make the angry person feel perceived as a *problem* to conquer instead of as a *person with a problem* to help resolve, you will cause more anger, not less.

A few years ago, I watched Gayle, a manager, respond to a client who called her a bitch by demanding that he not talk to her that way. The client retorted that he would talk to her any way he liked, which caused her to more forcefully demand that he stop. This, of course, made him respond more aggressively, thereby engaging in an increasingly vicious shouting match that was moving toward a physical confrontation. I stepped in, telling them we could resolve the issue, but first they both had to stop yelling at each other. They stopped and the crisis was averted, until Gayle had to have the last word by adding, "It's good that we are no longer yelling, but you should never talk to a manager that way." She *had* to have the last word, because she had learned to base her self-esteem on her authority and allowing someone to disrespect that authority decimated her self-esteem. Her underlying need to not let someone yell at her blinded her to the harm her words would cause: the client lunged at her in rage rather than accept her criticism and further "lose face" (having already lost some of his dignity upon reluctantly giving in to my request to stop arguing).

No one, including this manager, should have to take being verbally or physically abused. However, the manner in which you do not take it—whether you dispassionately defuse the person's anger or are provoked into overreacting—determines if you get the person to abate the abusive anger or escalate it. When ordering a person to "get out of my face" or "stop giving me the finger" brings your own inner needs and issues into the relationship, your intervention becomes more about you and less about letting the person know her abuse is unacceptable. The abuse can be real and has to be addressed, but your first task should be to defuse the situation rather than react out of being disrespected. You need to be able to "talk down" the belligerent person or set limits to someone's ranting and do so out of a calm intervention rather than out of a need to ensure she knows she cannot disrespect you. The former responds *to* the person's anger and leads to de-escalating it while the latter—"You are not going to call me a bitch"—reacts *out of* fight/flight/counter-transference and usually results in an escalated "But you are a bitch, bitch!" You will regret that you did not more calmly respond to the person's anger when now you have a more intense and intrusive anger to manage. The earlier discussed receptionist Bonnie and manager Gayle realized this when their clients' anger intensified and they were no longer responding to them out of maintaining their authority but instead out of anxiety.

You would probably recognize a defensive approach to a person's anger if you saw someone else doing it. You might note that if he had not "talked down" to the incensed person or had allowed her to "save face" then she would not have become angrier. Another victim of verbal abuse might not have seen that the irate individual simply needed to vent her feelings when it was obvious to everyone else that it was not personal. You can recognize the direct affect a person's temper tantrum or cursing has on you and on the way it elicits your response to it. You can see it in your interaction with a person whose angry sense of entitlement "pushes your buttons" or whose yelling makes you yell back rather than remain calm. You can recognize it when your response is more aggressive than it should be, your tone is too strident for the situation or your delivery is judgmental instead of responsive.

Before you even begin to deal with others' anger, ask yourself what you know of your own. You might be surprised by what you discover. You might think you are generally peaceful but find yourself becoming inexplicably upset when confronted by certain situations. Or you might have always thought of yourself as possessing endless patience but somehow certain people "get to you" more quickly than you thought possible and you find yourself aggressively acting out of character. We will see that angry people have an uncanny ability to recognize these "buttons" in others and trigger them.

The previously mentioned manager Gayle would neither have overreacted when the incensed client did not respect her authority nor been unprepared for his assault if she was aware of both her own underlying need not to have her authority disrespected and its resulting negative influence on her intervention. Know yourself and what emotions and needs you bring to defusing an angry person. Is your first response to someone's yelling or rage *Oh no, not another person who cannot control his temper!* Do you immediately try to stifle a person's outburst? Do you feel that previously defined physical manifestation of fight/flight: tenseness, rapid breathing, sweaty palms, etc.? Do you say to yourself, *I'm not going to let her talk to me that way?*

Recognizing the "buttons" an angry person pushes within you and the way they affect your intervention allows you to adjust your response: "I frequently get defensive when someone is angry at me so I am going to try to be more open to what he is saying." "I don't understand why I always overreact to being yelled at, but I am not going to do it this time." Or you recognize that a person's inflammatory "you idiot" pushes your buttons and causes you to immediately declare, "No one calls me an idiot!" Knowing this allows you to stay calm and examine the situation, whereby you might understand the person's angry slur is not the personal attack you *felt* it to be. "I hate being called an idiot, but he is just letting off steam, so I am not going to let it get to me."

Let's revisit Bonnie, the receptionist who was verbally abused and ultimately physically hurt by the client Tom. She could have stopped his angry ascent into violence if she had first stopped her instinctual reaction to his anger. She was correct that she was simply doing her job and should not be disrespected, but if she had told herself to remain calm and, as we will examine, out of that calm was able to recognize the degree of Tom's anger and how her reaction to it was escalating rather than defusing it, she could have intervened in a manner that effectively abated his anger and protected her from further verbal and ultimately physical abuse: *Tom is getting more upset with me when I tell him to stop yelling, but it's only because he needs his medication and so I have to somehow let him know I am on his side.*

Responding to someone's yelling or cursing for what it is rather than for the buttons it pushes within you does not mean you do not address the person's inappropriate behavior, nor does it imply you no longer have buttons to be pushed. It is not immature or unprofessional to have buttons, nor to have them pushed. We all have them; some are more quickly activated and others require more circumspect circumstances to make them known. The problem is not that we have buttons but that we might deny them. If we ignore the fact that we have less patience with certain people or that a particular behavior or attitude really "gets under our skin," these buttons are more easily triggered. You instead want to be aware of buttons such that even if you are not entirely in control of the underlying issues they represent then at least you are sufficiently aware so as to not let them become entangled in your response to the angry person. As a result you will be less fettered by your own needs and better prepared to use the techniques we will now examine to defuse a person's anger.

At last, you might be saying to yourself, *we are now going to deal with real de-escalation issues.* You might be thinking that too much discussion has been given to recognizing and managing your internal response to the person yelling at you when the real problem is *the person yelling at you.* Be assured, however, when you learn the techniques to defuse the hostile or enraged person that you will appreciate both the importance of how to apply these techniques and learning the effect your response has on how successful they will be.

IDENTIFY AND CALM YOUR ANGER

How you react to anger greatly affects your ability to defuse another person's anger. Do you react to anger with your own warning signs of growing anger?

- Flushed face
- Tense muscles
- Pounding heart
- Warm or hot body temperature
- Pacing
- Stomping
- Talking loudly and/or quickly
- Restlessness
- Clenched jaw or fists
- Contemplating revengeful or enraged thoughts (e.g., *He's doing this to me intentionally. I'm going to get back at them for this. I would love to just explode. She is purposely trying to make me look like an idiot.*)

Take some time to learn your personal "onset symptoms" of anger. What are your personal "buttons" that people often push? Use past situations where you reacted with anger to help you compile your list. Practice identifying these warning signs of anger in yourself when you find yourself in heated situations.

- Create a strategy for remaining calm the next time you encounter an angry person:
- What are some ways you can react to angry people that are calm and constructive? Think of several for various situations.
- What are the most effective ways for you to relax and calm down? Explore some new methods of maintaining calm.
- Consider a time when you successfully remained calm while dealing with an angry person. What factors in the situation contributed to your calmness?

- Reflect on times you have observed others dealing with angry people. How did they react to the angry people? Were their strategies effective? See if you can implement methods used by the people who successfully played it cool into your own plan to remain calm.

CHAPTER 2:

Listening to Frustration

A person has been yelling or cursing and you have succeeded in not overreacting, but you become a bit annoyed when your composure does not temper her anger. You begin to question the earlier touted benefit of staying calm when it seems to have no effect on defusing the person's verbal abuse. The benefit, however, is that although staying calm did not automatically abate her anger, it did not escalate it, which would happen if you reacted aggressively. By staying calm you can truly *listen* to what makes her angry, which *does* defuse it.

Listening

You refrained from defensively reacting to the irate person but now, counter-intuitively, you have to restrain the seemingly natural inclination to tell her how to resolve the situation that made her agitated in the first place. What you need to do instead is first listen.

People frequently are angry, because they do not feel heard. They are denied something, disrespected or in some way slighted and yell in order to get their points across or curse in order to get your attention. Their anger is not a persistent part of their personalities, as we will see in later stages with people who are always

mean or easily enraged. Anger at this stage does not make you feel
blamed for the person's problems: "Why did you do this to me?",
or verbally attacked: "You bitch!", nor does it feel threatening: "If
you don't fix this you will regret it!" Anger at this early onset is in
response to a particular situation that frustrates people and when
the frustration is gone, the anger dissipates as well. It is a way of
standing up for themselves: not to stand belligerently over you, but
to ensure you see them and hear their frustration.

How do you defuse the irate person who yells at you because
he wants you to know he is frustrated or has been wronged? How
do you get him to calm down, to literally sit down as he is frantically
pacing, when his anger energizes him to stand up for himself rather
than passively accept being ignored?

First, what you do *not* do is stifle his feelings. Do not order
the angry person to stop yelling or say, "You can't talk to me that
way!" Reading this might make *you* want to yell at me: "Here I am
trying to help this person and he is cursing me. Am I supposed to
be a doormat, allowing this screaming banshee to walk all over
me?" Of course not. No one likes to be yelled at or disrespected,
nor should anyone have to take it. It feels horrible to be called des-
picable racial/gender slurs or to have someone scream at you and
it is natural to want to tell the person to back off or stop swearing:
"I will not take being called that!" "Don't point that finger at me!"

This reaction is understandable, but it is a mistake. You think
you need to quickly subdue someone's anger, to squash the
shouting or let the person know you will not tolerate cursing. But
ordering the person to stop yelling or swearing at this early stage
will make her angrier. It might work if you are a police officer and
your command to stop shouting carries the weight of your weapon
or ability to make an arrest. Or if you are a muscular bouncer at a
bar and no one wants to get *you* mad. But police officers are usually
trained to "talk down" an angry person rather than try to force him
with their authority or they soon develop the skills to do so, because
they learn that ordering a person to stop being angry can escalate
his anger and it is preferable to deal with him verbally rather than

forcefully. Even bouncers know there is always someone who thinks he can "take you", especially when he is under the influence of alcohol or drugs.

Most of us are neither muscular bouncers nor police officers and so do not carry this weight of authority that makes an irate person back down upon command. Just the opposite: You order an angry person to stop yelling or to "get out of my face" and she becomes angrier. She is not prepared for your critical reactions when, as discussed earlier, all she wants with her yelling is to be heard. She becomes angrier because telling a person who yells to get you to listen that she needs to stop yelling will not only frustrate her need to be heard but also is proof that you are not listening to her.

Furthermore, it is very difficult for an irate individual to stop being angry simply because you tell her to stop yelling. Remember, anger compels the person to stand up rather than be passive and to loudly let you know that she will not accept being ignored or that you need to hear an injustice that has to be rectified. Why should an angry person stop being angry solely based on the fact that you ordered him to stop cursing when he has good reason to be angry and knows from experience it is sometimes the only way to get people to hear him?

You might agree that ordering a person to stop yelling can be counterproductive, but it may seem to you that at least telling the agitated person to "calm down" should be beneficial. It would help restore the equanimity from which you will be able to better resolve what is upsetting the individual. But the person's escalated angry state makes him hear "calm down" as your trying to stifle what he feels—feelings that are real and should not be stifled. He is agitated and demanding for a reason. To the angry individual, telling him to calm down means that you have not heard he has a reason for being agitated, because otherwise you would not tell him to calm down. The latter comes across as not only ignoring his anger, but also trying to control what he feels and no one—including you and me—likes that. He might be the angry one, but you are seen as the aggressor, the one who is attempting to stifle his feelings or expropriate his control. And so he becomes angrier, not less angry. This is something I have seen over and over: What begins as a person shouting to get your attention or swearing out of frustration—what should have been defused by letting the person know you are listening, as we will shortly examine—instead escalates into louder and more aggressive shouting in order to be heard over the loudness of your demand to stop yelling: "Oh yeah? I will yell all I want! Try to stop me!" or "Don't' tell me to calm down! You calm down!" In other situations, he may become quiet by suppressing his anger, by cursing you under his breath, thereby letting his anger simmer until it boils over into rage, as we will see in a later chapter.

Asking the agitated person, "What's *your* problem" similarly does not make her think you are actually interested in hearing her problem. Saying, "Don't talk to me with that tone" does not make her believe you are trying to get her to lower her voice so you can understand her. Your words—especially when infused with earlier discussed counter-transference/adrenaline-driven defenses—make her feel ordered, criticized or even verbally attacked. Many times I have watched people judgmentally say, "You have no right to be angry" or sarcastically state, "What do you have to complain about?" The person does not demurely respond, "You're right; I have nothing to be angry about", especially when she has something that compels her to yell in frustration. Rather than quieting down, she will more forcefully express her feelings in order to let you know she will not passively accept being told not to express them: "What's my problem? I'll tell you my problem: you're my problem!" "*You* don't have to take this kind of crap? What kind of crap do you think *I'm* taking?"

You should not be surprised when people whose anger could have been defused by listening, which now will be discussed, instead yell louder because you do not listen. Your tendency is to do the same, to think if you can only get the person to hear you then you can get him to stop yelling and so you raise your voice to be heard over his. But you will lose this cacophonous contest, because as important as it might be to you to let him know he cannot yell at you, it is more important to him to let you know he will not be ignored or have his feelings stifled. He will raise the ante of anger by raising the tenor of his voice and, if the contest continues into a spiraling shouting match, will eventually no longer merely yell out of frustration, but rather out of later stage hostility that forces you to listen.

Think of the childhood rhyme "Sticks and stones may break my bones but names will never hurt me." While it might be true that "names will never hurt me" (at least not physically), it is also true that the offensive "name calling"—e.g., the racial/gender slur that did not get you to listen, as was its intention, can as a result harden into the more forceful "sticks and stones" that "may break my bones." Heidi, a social worker I supervised, ordered a client, Frank, to stop talking to her disrespectfully. Frank was upset because Heidi would not give him a hotel voucher and so he said, "Are you some stuck up bitch who lives in a big house and doesn't care that I sleep on the street?" Note he did not directly say "you bitch", which would have made it a personal verbal attack and more hostile. He instead yelled at her out of frustration, trying to get her to understand his situation. Her ordering him to stop cursing was further proof she was not listening and did not care. He became angrier as a result, aggressively replying "Make me" to Heidi's order to stop disrespecting her, to which she said, "Don't tempt me!" Frank then said he would tempt her, to which she said he better not.

This was no longer about de-escalation, about getting the client to calm down, and instead had turned into a contest to see who would back down first. The client was ready to take it to the next stages if necessary, to becoming belligerent and threatening. Heidi was not going to relent and was determined to win by asserting her authority to make him stop shouting. Frank threatened her—"You better give me that voucher if you know what is good for you"—to which she said she would not take being threatened and so would call the police. Frank hit her before she could call. In the end, Heidi lost to Frank's anger.

This incident should not have been about Heidi's feeling

disrespected. It should have been about defusing Frank's anger. But because it was not and instead was an attempt to stifle the client's anger due to Heidi's own need not to be cursed at, the result was an escalation of Frank's anger that ultimately ended in violence. Heidi was right that she should not take another person's abuse. She was wrong, however, in the way she told him. We will later examine how people in Heidi's situation—and you in similar verbally abusive scenarios—need to find the balance between listening to a person's anger and not taking the abuse that comes with that anger, which is a seminal yet sticky task. In later stages of anger, where intimidation is exerted and violence becomes likely, you will need to have more concern with immediately constraining someone's "sticks and stones" and protecting yourself. But at this less confrontational name-calling stage, you need to address a person's anger in a way that does not escalate it by responding to verbal abuse with demands that come across as your own verbal abuse or by reacting to disrespect by being disrespectful as well.

Ordering an angry person to stop yelling or cursing makes her yell or curse more, because it confronts *how* she expresses her feelings when you instead need to address the *what* of her anger. Yelling or cursing is *how* the person expresses *what* angers her. She is upset, because she feels slighted or ignored and so she yells. The latter is meant to get you to focus on the former and when instead it gets you to clamp down on the yelling, it makes the person think not only are you further ignoring her feelings but also are trying to stifle them. By concentrating on the yelling and how to abate it, you lose focus on what the anger is about and how to defuse it. The irate person becomes louder or bolder *because* you judged or tried to stop it rather than listened to what caused it. The resulting "Stop yelling at me," as we will see it unfold with Heidi's response to the disgruntled and disrespectful Frank, is met with "Make me" which is met with "I'll call the police" which is met with "Go ahead" and so on and so forth.

Become less focused on how the person gives voice to her frustration and instead listen to what makes her angry. She might be wrong—or at least inappropriate—in the way she yells or curses you, but listen because it expresses what she feels. She might call you an ugly name or slam the door and you respond as if it is a personal attack when instead—at least at this early stage—it is simply an attempt to get you to listen. If you say to yourself "I don't have to put up with this" or "No one talks to me that way", you are not only closing yourself to hearing what the person's anger is saying, but also as a result you are aggressively responding to her anger in a way that escalates rather than defuses it.

I was waiting in line at a store when I observed the clerk, Heather, being mistreated by a rude customer. After the harangue had finished and the customer walked away in a huff, I asked Heather how she was able to manage the rude customer. She said it was part of her job, but that particular man had brought her close to telling him to shut up. She knew from experience, however, that being brusque would exacerbate his anger and so instead suppressed "telling him off." It also helped restrain her instincts when she told herself that perhaps the customer was not really a bad person and was simply having a bad day. Confronting his rudeness, she further knew, would only contribute to making his bad day worse thereby making his rudeness more abrasive. Then she would have serious trouble, because his anger would no longer be the expression of a frustrating day—an anger she new how to defuse—and instead would escalate into a hostility that would be more difficult to calm.

I asked Heather how she knew this customer's anger was simply an expression of a bad day as opposed to that of a bad person. She said the latter's anger would be directly aimed at her—"you bitch"—which would have made it personal and would have made her feel anxious. Instead, this person's anger was an expression of what she probably would have felt if she was in a similarly frustrating situation. Knowing what it would take to calm her own frustration, she knew if she was attentive to the angry customer and listened to his complaint that he would become less obstreperous and generally more responsive to her entreaties.

The store clerk's response to the rude customer reminds me of a former boss who similarly was short-tempered when she was having a bad day. She was normally a relaxed person but sometimes she inexplicably became ornery or easily agitated. Like Heather, I recognized that my boss's anger was not personally aimed at me nor was it vicious. Also akin to the store clerk, I did not confront her anger (which could have jeopardized my job, as it could have done with the store clerk since "the customer is always right"). I instead stayed detached and gave her the space to be frustrated. The result usually was that she eventually let go of her frustration and even sometimes apologized and said she was having a bad day.

Listen to the angry person. You will hear that her cursing is not vicious or her slamming the door is not hostile (as you will recognize them to be in later stages). In actuality, these acts are meant to get you to hear her. Listening to what angers her rather than responding to how she expresses it lets the person know that her goal to get you to hear her anger and your goal are the same. You both want to address what upsets her rather than stifle or exacerbate it. She thereby will no longer need to yell in order to be heard, because now she feels she is heard: "I can certainly see why that would make you angry." "No wonder you are so upset." Or as the store clerk would say, "Looks like you might be having a bad day. How can I help to make it better?"

Tom, who was late to his doctor's appointment, yelled at Bonnie, the receptionist, because he needed her to hear that the medicine was important to him and he would have quieted his yelling if the receptionist had listened to him. Frank, the client who became embroiled in a shouting match with the social worker, Heidi, would have also calmed down if Heidi had allowed him to vent his frustration rather than order him to stop shouting. This does not mean Bonnie and Heidi should have ignored *how* the anger of these people was being expressed but—unlike in later stages where it is more disruptive and even dangerous and so strict limits need to be set, as we will examine—at this early stage the anger was mostly a means to get attention or to vent frustration and would dissipate once having done so.

Okay, you say, you will listen to *what* angered the person rather than tell her to stop yelling and you will give her insights into how to resolve it. Sorry, as much as the latter seems reasonable, one of the first tasks of listening is not to talk. The person expressing anger needs you to listen and therefore giving her advice means you are not listening. It makes her feel you are one more person telling her what to do—as well meaning as it is. To her, you are one more person who does not know why she is upset, because you are too busy talking to hear what she is saying.

I have seen people think they could calm angry people down by trying to help them understand the misperceptions or miscommunications that lead to being angry in spite of the fact that the more they talked about what went wrong, the more irritated the other people became. These people found it incomprehensible that their perfectly logical explanation did not diffuse the people's anger. Any reasonable person would appreciate their insight and find in it the guidance to resolve what was frustrating to them. But what they failed to remember is that an escalated emotional state makes a person less reasonable. They should not have been surprised when the angry people did not respond positively to their persuasive reasoning and instead aggressively interjected, "Would you stop talking for a second and just listen to me?"

The person who is yelling to get you to listen does not become less angry—nor receptive to what you have to say—if she does not first think you have heard what she has to say. She instead regards your advice as more about you than her, as if you are more interested in making her know what *you* think makes her angry rather than hearing what she *knows* makes her angry. She is trying to get you to know too if only you would listen. "Why are you saying that? Tell me something I don't know!" That is why Tom felt angrier when he told Bonnie he needed his medication and she reiterated that he missed his appointment: "You're not hearing me—I need my medicine!" That is why Frank became deeper embroiled in the shouting match with Heidi. His yelling was not about disrespecting her and instead was utilized in order to get her to listen to him. When she told him to stop disrespecting her he became more aggressive, saying in a way, "This is not about you—it's about me!"

So "bite your tongue" and first listen to the angry person. Let her talk and express her feelings before you offer your opinion, otherwise no one is listening to anyone and the only direction of that conversation is increased frustration.

Active Listening

To "bite your tongue" rather than tell the angry person what to do creates the impression you are listening but it does not *necessarily* mean you are listening. You might refrain from talking, but you can be preoccupied with other thoughts or with planning your response rather than listening. The irate person probably knows when you are only superficially listening and will become angrier. My friend John's wife, Anna, frequently complained that John was only apparently listening to whatever was frustrating her, because in spite of his saying "I see" or "of course you are right", as soon as the conversation was concluded he was immediately talking about something new, having been mentally involved in that new subject while listening to her talk about her problems. Now what frustrates Anna includes the concept that John really does not listen even when he says he is.

Listening makes the irate person feel heard when it involves more than simply *not* talking and instead includes being attentive and receptive. This is called active listening. It is often expressed as "Do you feel me?" Do you *really* get what the person is saying and not just appear to do so? We will take a moment to examine what makes active listening "get" the person's anger and how it helps defuse it.

Active listening is a method of listening that is based entirely on focusing and understanding what the other person is saying on both an emotional and cognitive level. This means listening to the angry person is not always agreeing, not always affirmatively nodding your head or saying "uh huh" or "mmhmm, mmhmm." It instead requires you to make the effort to understand the person and to make her feel understood.

You demonstrate active listening by being attentive. Let the angry person know she has your full attention. Let her know this in several ways, such as good eye contact, a concerned look on your face or with the sensitive way you ask questions related to her frustrations. You demonstrate your attentiveness as well by what you should *not* be doing: rolling your eyes or frowning when the person says something that is unusual, mumbling disapproval under your breath, tapping your fingers, looking at your watch, interrupting her to say something or to talk with someone else, looking around, appearing distracted or disinterested.

Impatience with the irate person is a sure way to announce you are not attentive and to escalate her anger. Maybe her frustration makes it difficult to clearly communicate her feelings, but you are busy and so you want her to get to the point. Maybe in her escalated emotional state she is less "reachable" or logical and is more prone to being agitated than to talking with you. Remind yourself to be patient with the angry person. Do not hurry her when she does not immediately respond to your listening; hurrying makes her feel judged for being too slow or stupid and reinforces that you are not listening.

I have observed too many people who felt slighted, because they were hurried when they were trying to explain what frustrated them, they felt ignored when they were trying to get a worker's attention or they were made to wait too long in reception areas. The anger of these people would have been lessened if someone had given them the individual attention that made them feel they mattered. How many times have all of us been in lines or at events waiting for something to begin and became agitated because no one in authority had the decency at least to inform us of the delay? Make sure you do not make an angry person feel this way. Be patiently attentive to her—"It's okay, take your time"—which reduces her frantic sense of urgency and helps her feel less anxious about communicating her feelings. If the angry person has to wait—which you never want to make her do, but sometimes by necessity happens— at least make her feel less invisible, less a faceless number or just another person and less frustrated by treating her respectfully as an individual. If not, you will regret you were not more patient or did not take the time to defuse her agitation when it was at this more manageable frustration stage.

Also remember that being attentive is not only patiently listening to what the angry person says but also listening to what she does not say. Be attentive to her non-verbal communication, which can clearly express the intensity of her anger. Pay attention to her tone of voice, to whether her speech is rapid or pressured. Take note whether she appears nervous, scared or frightened. Does she seem to be in control of her anger or is she dangerously close to "losing it"? Is she responsive to your attempts to work with her or is she demanding, blaming everyone and taking no responsibility? Do drugs seem to have a part in her agitation; does she appear to be mentally unstable?

Also take note of your surroundings and of what is going on around the aggravated person. Be aware of how hot it is in the room, which can add to a person's discomfort and thereby make her more upset. Is the room too noisy or maybe there are too many people in it? Either can lead to greater agitation. Be aware of those people who are with the angry person. They might contribute to her agitation, bringing with them the peer pressure that compels her to act on anger rather than back down from it. In the opposite way, they might be of some help in calming her.

Besides being attentive to the incensed person and her environment, be attentive to yourself. You will be of little help to the irate individual if you recognize the numerous factors that contribute to her anger but are blind to aspects of yourself that make her angry. You will have greater success in calming the irritated person if *your* demeanor is calm (which, as said earlier, hopefully models to the person how to handle the situation more calmly). This helps her know you are neither overreacting defensively to her anger nor getting "caught up" in its urgency.

Be aware of your tone of voice, whether it is soothing and reassuring or imperious and confrontational. Similarly notice if you are talking rapidly, which might reflect your own nervousness and which will probably irritate the frustrated person. Notice your body language, whether your arms are folded defensively or you appear tense. You might not be aware that your physical appearance is not aligned with how you are talking to the person. That is, you might be speaking calmly but your body speaks of being confrontational. If the presence of others can have a direct effect on the angry person, they can have an effect on your response to her. They can make you feel that you are being judged in the way you handle the situation or make you feel embarrassed being cursed in front of others when you instead feel you should have the situation under control.

You can adjust your physical appearance when you realize you are coming across aggressively or defensively. Establish better eye contact so that it is less accusatory, lower you tone of voice so that it is more reassuring and calming, unfold your arms and slow your speech so as to convey a sense of normalcy rather than stress. The earlier discussed Gayle, who ordered the person to stop yelling, might have noticed she was wagging her finger judgmentally at him and noticed its negative effect—"You better stop shaking your finger at me"—and thereby helped calm the situation by stopping her finger pointing. Any of these acts of self-awareness will contribute to making the aggravated person feel less angry. They also contribute to opening the way for the next step in actively listening to the irate person, which is acknowledging the person's anger.

Acknowledge Anger

The person who yells to make you listen will stop yelling when you listen and will become even less angry when he knows you *heard* his anger. That is, attentive listening is more than not talking so the person can speak and more than a mere cognitive recording of what he says so as to recite it back word for word. It is letting the person know you hear what angers him and that you take it seriously: "I can see why this upsets you."

It might not seem like such a significant act, but I have found that letting the person know you "get" his anger is one of the most important tools in de-escalation. He yells and, in anticipation of being told to stop yelling, is ready to yell even louder; you break this cycle if instead of confronting his anger you acknowledge it: "If it happened to me, I'd be angry too." This tells the person you know he has a reason to be angry and you are neither going to rebuke him for it nor let it get in the way of trying to understand his situation. He will let go of some of his anger when he feels you are listening to what made him upset and will become even calmer when he realizes that not only are you not censoring his anger but also that you take it seriously.

Bart, one of my clients, was angry at Social Security, because he did not receive his benefit check. Robin, his social worker, listened to him and thought she could calm Bart down by letting him know he did not have to be so upset, because his situation was manageable: "Don't worry about it—I'll look into it." Saying, "You don't have to worry about it" or "it's not so bad" are common responses to an irate person. They are meant to be reassuring to the agitated individual, to let him know his situation is not as bad as he imagined and so he can relax a little. The problem is that he might think his situation *is* as bad as he imagined, that he has good reason to be agitated and how dare he be told otherwise. Bart was dumbfounded when told not to worry, because Robin obviously did not understand that not only did he not get his check but also he has no money to pay rent. "Don't worry? Easy for you to say! It's not you who is going to lose his housing!" Or more succinctly and angrily: "You just don't get it!"

He is right! You do not intend to trivialize a person's frustration when you say it's "not that bad" but it can be "that bad" to him. This is why using humor to defuse anger can be delicate. Occasionally saying something lighthearted might ease tension as well as might demonstrate you are not anxious and are handling the situation with equanimity. More frequently, however, humor will be misinterpreted as not taking the person seriously. You may also come across as minimizing the person's feelings when you try to raise his spirits with a cheerleading pep talk or a trite "You'll be fine." All of this is like being told, "Don't worry—be happy." Now the angry person has something else to worry about besides what initially angered him: you're trying to abate his anger without understanding why he should be angry. Saying, "Hey, it's a gorgeous day so let's not argue" probably will result in a response such as, "Oh yeah? What's gorgeous about it? You aren't the one who didn't..."

Before you tell the angry person "take it easy", make sure he knows not only that you are listening to what angers him but also that you take the problem seriously. The seemingly supportive "No problem; I'm here to help" is not helpful, because the person does not hear the offer of help due to being incensed about you not listening to him, as evidenced by prefacing your offer by saying there is no problem when there is a problem. That is why Tom became angrier at Bonnie in the earlier mentioned missed doctor appointment situation when she tried to explain why his medicine was unavailable without *first* acknowledging the frustration that made him feel this way. She should have preceded her explanation about the doctor being gone with, "I'm sorry, I know the medicine is important to you." Letting the person know you are listening to what he says *and* you understand his frustration defuses his yelling, because yelling at this stage is intended to get you to listen to what angers him. Now that the person knows you not only hear his frustration but also take it seriously, he does not have to yell anymore.

Consider yourself in the position of Robin talking with Bart, who did not receive his Social Security benefits. If you offer an explanation into what happened in the belief that it will calm his frustration instead of first acknowledging the intensity of his feelings, you will make him think you are ignoring his feelings. "Social Security made a mistake, but you don't have to worry, because we can fix it." Your offer to fix the problem would be reassuring to a clear-headed person but will not defuse this person's anger. He is irate *because* Social Security made a mistake and so to be told they made a mistake but it can be fixed—as if that makes it better—makes it worse. Social Security still made a mistake that negatively affected him. Instead, let the person know you hear his anger before you offer solutions to the problem that angered him. This will calm him before any explanation will do so. "Of course you're angry about not getting your check; I'd be, too. I think I know the mistake they made so we can try to fix it."

Leo told his friend Jason about being fired from his job for disagreeing with his boss. Jason thought he was offering constructive insight when he said to Leo, "You should not have told your boss she was wrong." This is probably true, but in his angry state Leo felt judged: "You're saying I don't know my job?" Jason never said or even implied that Leo did not know his job but that is what Leo heard, because in his aggravation what he needed at that moment was a "sympathetic ear" and anything short of that—as constructive as it may have seemed to Jason—was taken as criticism. Leo first needed to hear "Sorry you were fired" or "That's crazy that your boss could not take constructive advice," which would acknowledge why he was angry. He would be more open to addressing what concretely happened after he knows his friend understands what he felt.

An example is the common anger-inducing occurrence of a person who accidentally bumps into someone else. The angry person yells, "Watch where you're going" and you the bumper say, "Take it easy" or "It was an accident." The bumped person does not want to hear "take it easy" when his drink was knocked out of his hand or he has been hurt, even if it was an accident. What he first needs to hear is concern for the trouble or hurt inflicted on him, even if it was unintentional. Without this, he hears your logical explanation—"it was just an accident"—*not* as an explanation but as an excuse, as a way of not taking responsibility. If you instead precede your explanation with a sincere "sorry", you would make the person feel you were concerned for what you accidentally caused. This would help defuse the bumped person's instinctual reaction to being bumped, making him more receptive to the subsequent explanation that it was an accident and further dissipate his irritation.

The explanation following the apology or acknowledgment

should not be preceded by saying "but", as in "I'm sorry, but it was an accident." The word "but" can make the person feel you are excusing or even retracting your words of support. State the apology and stop. *Then* offer an explanation: "I'm sorry. I didn't mean to bump into you."

Be careful of the tone of voice in your apology. You might only grudgingly offer an apology, because it *really* was an accident and you think the person is overreacting or being childish. The aggravated person will likely recognize the criticism behind your tone and become angrier.

A person who is upset because of a mistake you made will similarly become angrier if you try to explain what happened without first being apologetic. It comes across as trying to justify the mistake (as well as ignoring the frustration it caused). "It's simply a mistake; it's not as if I did it on purpose." This will probably result in an acrimonious "Yes you did" or "Are you calling me a liar?" The result will be escalated anger, so acknowledge the mistake and offer an apology before you proceed to explain the circumstances. This will also create the impression that in spite of your mistake you are trustworthy. The person has less reason to be angry when some of that anger was based on not being able to trust that you are truly listening to what upsets him.

Even if you did not make a mistake, at least say you can see why the person is angry and that you are sorry for how it makes him feel. You can also apologize for another's mistake when the person is yelling at you about it, as with Bart, the earlier discussed client who was angry about not receiving his Social Security check. What the social worker should have said was, "I'm sorry for what Social Security did." This not only demonstrates she knows what happened is a hardship for Bart, but also helps deflect some of Bart's anger away from her.

However, do not appear to be blaming the party to whom you are redirecting the person's ire: "Don't yell at me; it's their fault!" Blaming others can make you look like you are trying to escape responsibility and can also appear to be encouraging anger rather than defusing it. When responding to the person who says, "That *jerk* at Social Security did not give me my check", saying, "Yeah, she is a jerk" acknowledges his feelings but also stimulates his anger or makes him think it is acceptable to be mean. Instead say, "I don't know if she is a jerk, but I can see why you are angry," which is supportive of the person's feelings but does not enflame them.

Empathy

I have frequently heard people who have been cursed or yelled at state they would not say "sorry" when they had nothing to do with the people's anger. They are the innocent victims of verbal abuse and so why should they say they are sorry?

The answer is empathy, which reinforces your listening. It makes the irate person know you not only hear her frustration but also have some *feeling* for her experience and you hold her best interests in your response. It does this because empathy is what makes you take the other person's perspective, to "walk in her shoes" and thereby to be more sensitive to what she is feeling.

Empathy is to ask yourself, "Wouldn't I be just as angry if that happened to me?" We have a tendency not to think or feel this way, because when someone yells at us we go into the earlier discussed myopic fight/flight response. To prevent this defensive curtailing of empathy, first try to see the situation from the irate person's perspective. Subsequently ask yourself what it would take to defuse the situation if you were that person.

Imagine what you would feel if you did not get paid and could not pay the monthly rent or mortgage. *Now* respond to the person who is yelling about not getting his Social Security check. You would probably be more understanding of his frustration as well as to his agitated response to your suggestion that he "take it easy." This does not mean you think his yelling or cursing is appropriate nor that you take responsibility for his anger. Empathy does not require you to agree with the person's anger, only that you try to grasp how he is feeling and how these feelings affect his dealing with the situation. Then let him know it: "I can see why this would upset you." "That really stinks." "I would be frustrated too."

Be careful how you let the angry person know you care. Never say, "I know how you feel." It seems patronizing. You and the frustrated person are separate individuals and you do not know his feelings exactly. You will probably get in response: "How could you know how I feel? You go home every day to your house while I have to sleep on the street." And try not to say, "It seems you are angry." The response will be, "It doesn't *seem* like I'm angry; I *am* angry!" Instead say something like "That's lousy" or "No wonder you're angry," thereby making the person feel you are understanding but are not presuming to know what he is experiencing.

An important aspect of empathizing with an angry person is that not only does it make him feel you are supportive but also you have established a non-threatening relationship with him. This is critical, because it makes you an ally in his attempt to overcome his frustration. His anger initially makes him approach you if not as the enemy then at least as one who withholds (or is capable of withholding) what he needs. Empathy counters this approach by showing you are on his side; that you are not against him but working with him. "I'm sorry it's been so difficult for you; let's figure out what we can do." Forming an alliance also critically makes you less susceptible to becoming the victim of an anger that could escalate into violence, since the angry person is less likely to be violent toward an ally. This is especially relevant if you are not able to give the person what he wants, because at least he will know it is not coming out of an authoritarian or punitive response. "Sorry, I wish I could do more."

Think of the earlier discussion of Tom who was late to his appointment to get his medication and became angry then hostile and violent when Bonnie, the receptionist, told him not to yell at her, because it was not her fault he was late. She was right that it was not her fault, but she also was wrong. She was wrong, as said earlier, because she was not listening to what upset him but also because she did not understand that in Tom's highly charged emotional state he did not hear, "You are late and the doctor is gone, that is why you cannot get your medicine." He instead heard, "You are late and you are being punished for it by not getting your medicine." Why else, in Tom's mind, would he be denied medicine that is much more important than the time? So before Bonnie addressed Tom's acrimonious demeanor she should have let him know she understood he was upset and even that she was sorry for the resulting frustration: "I know the medicine is important to you." This would have made him feel she cared and would have made him more receptive when she subsequently explained, "It is after hours and I wish there was something I could do, but the doctor is gone."

The bond you form in empathy can also be a kind of "quick fix" disarming of a person's anger. If you offer a glass of water to an aggravated person, for example, you show your concern and thereby make some kind of tenuous connection that helps to lower his guardedness. This connection is not a profound healing experience that eviscerates all his anger but simply allows for a momentary reprieve from his anger. It is at minimum a temporary "time-out" that restores some calm.

Taking a "time-out" is similar to the moratorium from anger you try to create when your attempts at defusing an irate individual seem dead-ended. "I think it would be best if we take a break for a moment and then come back to this." A couple I was counseling sometimes became seemingly inextricably stuck in their frustration with each other's communication (or lack thereof) until I reminded them that it was okay to step back from it—even though their issue was not resolved—and then return to their conversation with a little more calm. The suggestion of a break in itself was usually enough to bring them some relief.

Be careful when you say "I" when talking with an angry person, as in an empathetic "I'd be angry, too." It might be genuine and let the person know you understand, but it can lead to two potentially negative responses. First, the person can testily respond, "You could not possibly understand what I feel!" Second, saying "I" can make the frustrated person sense you have taken the focus away from his feelings and put it on yourself. Your response should not be how *you* understand the person's anger, because then it is about what you think of his experience as opposed to what he experiences. Instead put the focus on *his* experience. Rather than always saying, "I understand" say, "That's understandable."

Further, do not try too hard to convince the person you are empathetic. You might think you have to be positive, be upbeat or have a pleasant inflection in your voice and that will lift the person out of her frustration. Instead be real, be sincere, talk in a neutral tone and never voice your empathy in jargons or clichés such as "I feel your pain." If you do you might soon be *physically* feeling the pain that is inflicted on you as a result of making the angry person feel patronized and angrier.

Verbalize Anger

The clearest expression of empathy is a simple "How can I help you?" This question is a particularly good way to break through the person's angry expectation that you are going to respond to her anger with indifference if not criticism. It lets her know you want to resolve what angered her rather than simply address how she expresses it. So rather than telling the person how you are going to help, ask her to tell you how you can help. This will take you far in defusing the person whose yelling came from trying to make you listen but who now can stop yelling—or at least lower it—because she no longer has to yell to get your help. She now can talk to you in response to your question. Had the earlier discussed social worker Heidi who was embroiled in the shouting match with Frank said, "This yelling at each other is getting us nowhere. Please tell me what I can do to help you," Frank would no longer have felt the need to yell in order to get her to listen.

Sometimes it is aggravating that you have to ask the person yelling at you how you can help when it seems obvious to *you* that you are there to help—especially if you are a concerned friend or family member or are in a helping profession. Why is the person yelling when instead she could simply ask for assistance? Some people have difficulty asking for help. Maybe they never learned to communicate their needs or were taught being needy was unacceptable. Maybe they learned to become angry to attain what they want rather than to ask for it. And even if they communicate their feelings, many people's experience is that others—including service providers—are just as likely to deny what they need rather than help. These people often have or expect an adversarial relationship with you when they need your help.

Asking the irate person "How can I help you?" is also important, because it directs her communication away from yelling or cursing toward *telling* you what angered her. For example, you acknowledge Bart's feelings when he is angry at Social Security, because he was denied his benefit check. Then by asking, "How can I help you?" or "Why don't you tell me what happened?" you steer his anger away from screaming about what happened toward talking about it. The latter does not mean he is less angry, because he is still upset, but telling you why he is angry reduces the intensity of *how* he expresses his feelings and allows you to focus more on *what* angers him. When he replies, "You want to know what happened? I'll tell you what happened—the clerk at Social Security… " Notice he said he'll *tell* you what happened to anger him rather than yelled about it.

Keep in mind that the act of talking about what angers a person might make him angrier. It riles him to think about the injustice or the hurt inflicted on him and so he becomes more frustrated. As a result he might revert to yelling rather than continue to talk about what upset him. Should this happen, back away from whatever it is that agitates him. Reinforce you are listening and calmly repeat your offer of help. You can even remind him that talking more effectively communicated his needs than yelling. "I could understand you better when you were not shouting so let's see if we can get back to that."

Do not promise something you cannot provide when the person tells you how to help. "I will fix it for you" is very different from "I will do everything I can do to help." It might calm the person for the moment to say you will fix it but if you cannot fix it, you will exacerbate his anger.

Clarification

People usually are not going to immediately start talking about their anger rather than shouting it simply because you say "How can I help you?" Acknowledging their frustration makes them less upset, but emotions are still running high and therefore might interfere with clearly explaining what angers them. They might need assistance verbalizing the intense feelings they do not know how to put into words or only know how to express through yelling. Help people who have difficulty telling you what they feel by saying encouraging things such as, "I see what you mean. Why don't you tell me more?" Or ask questions that encourage talking about what is frustrating: "What happened to make you so angry?"

Be careful how you ask questions, however. For instance, do not ask, "Why are you angry?" or "Why did that happen?" Asking questions with *why* can make the person bring up more anger than you expect as he explains to you the motivation behind why someone slighted him or the reason he is susceptible to becoming upset over your interaction with him. It can also make him feel you are questioning his right to be angry, which happens when he hears your "why" questions not as a constructive inquiry into what happened to make him angry, but rather as an accusation. "Why should *you* be angry?" will not encourage talking about what angered him, but reinforce his yelling: "Because—that's why!" Instead ask the question, "What happened?" which encourages talking about the facts of the experience.

Further, do not ask yes or no questions. They will make the incensed person feel interrogated and his answers accordingly will be resistant and not informative. Instead, ask open-ended questions, inquiries that broaden your conversation beyond yes or no answers and that help the person discuss what actually happened. Rather than "Are you angry because you did not get your check?" which will elicit a simple "yes" or a more pointed, "Of course, you idiot," ask, "What happened that made you so angry?" which will hopefully solicit information about what happened and thereby open a conversation in which you become more knowledgeable about how to help the angry person.

You will also make the person feel more open to talking if your manner of responses to her begins with "I" rather than an inflammatory "you." No one likes being told "You have to…" or worse "You better not…" Instead of saying, "You are confusing me"—which the angry person interprets as blame—or "you better stop yelling right now"—which is interpreted as an order—say, "I am not sure if I understand."

You can similarly change the way you address the angry person from "you" to a more indirect "we": "Hey, why don't we both calm down and see if we can fix this." Saying "we" might irk you since you are not the one who needs to relax, but saying "we" rather than the more confrontational "you" avoids the latter's tendency to make the person feel judged or commanded. Using the word "we" also makes the angry person feel you are his ally and that you are acting with him as opposed to against him, as we discussed in the section on empathy.

If the person continues to be agitated and you cannot understand what she is saying, patiently help her communicate more clearly by asking her to slow down or to repeat what she said. I have often observed workers who did not comprehend an angry person's words but were too embarrassed or reluctant to ask the person to repeat it, as if doing so would aggravate the person, because it suggested they were not listening or were not smart enough to comprehend. It is easy, however, to misinterpret what people mean, especially when they are in an escalated state of anger and not communicating clearly.

Check your understanding of what the person is saying by briefly paraphrasing or restating what you understood him to say. This will prod the person to repeat it so both he and you are clear about it. "Let me be sure I've got this straight…" If you understand what the person is saying and want him to expound upon it, encourage more of it with an acknowledging "uh huh" or "Got it; why don't you tell me more?" But if the person defensively says you do not "get it," do not take it personally. It is not a verbal attack against you. You will know what a personal verbal attack feels like.

At this early stage of anger, the person is simply expressing the frustration of trying to get you to understand his feelings. Remind yourself that it is easier for the person to yell at you than to put the logical words together to explain why he is angry.

Getting the person to talk about anger not only helps to clarify feelings but also to focus them. Intense emotions can be confusing and lead to a sense of disconnected or scattered conversation. The person might seem to ramble aimlessly about what angered her or she talks in generalities—"those people"—that make it difficult to understand the specifics of the situation that angered her. She might also bring up unrelated grievances that upset her and that thwart her attempt to clearly communicate. Empathically acknowledge her feelings and then help her focus by moving her away from emotional expressions of anger to talking about the particulars of the problem that angered her. "I know you have a lot to be angry about, but I think we were on to something so let's get back to that for the moment."

Finally, just as you need to clarify what the angry person is saying so as not to misinterpret it, remember this person is in an intensely emotional state and can easily misinterpret what you say. Answer any questions honestly, without equivocation. Do not try to conceal something or say, "It's too complicated to explain." The person probably will say, "You really don't know what's going on anyway!" And never say "Because that's the way it is!" How often have we seen a person yell something like, "Why can't I see my records?" and a worker respond, "Because that is the rule." It makes the person angrier.

Tell the person if you do not know what is transpiring: "I am not sure I understand it myself, but give me a chance to see if I can explain it to you." Or more simply, "I really don't know; sorry." And even if a person's questions seem irrational or silly, make sure you answer them or at least acknowledge them; otherwise she will feel ignored. Do not give long answers, because anger shortens a person's attention span. Be concise and use simple, non-complicated language. "You have every right to be angry" is preferable to

"Their inconsideration of your obvious needs is unacceptable and explains why you should feel incensed!" The latter can make the person feel stupid, especially if in her heightened emotions she does not understand what you are saying or thinks you are trying to make her feel stupid; the result will be more anger.

When you finish responding to what the angry person tells you, listen patiently and be supportive of what she says. In this way you will have helped her clarify and talk about what upset her and thus will have moved closer to defusing her anger. This would have been the outcome had Bonnie told Tom she was sorry that he could not get his medication after listening attentively to why it caused him to be so angry. This response would have made him feel he was being heard and thereby given him less reason to yell about his frustration.

Problem Solving

Helping the person talk about what angered her rather than shouting does not mean her anger is gone. Remember that Tom's anger at the receptionist would have dissipated with her acknowledgement of his feelings and subsequent explanation of what happened. But he still would have been frustrated, because he did not get what he wanted. "Okay, but what does that have to do with getting my medicine?" You need more than insights into *why* something happens to ultimately defuse the person's anger. You need to provide insights into *how* they can work at resolving what angered them. This requires problem solving skills. You no longer simply listen to or are empathetic with the person and instead give advice about what angered her and direction toward fixing it. You initially refrained from making suggestions, because the person first needed you to listen; now that he knows you have heard him and tried to understand his frustration, he is less resistant to hearing what you have to say.

The final de-escalation task of early stage anger is helping the person find a better way of *dealing* with frustration than the angry way she first chose to deal with it. People frequently become angry because they feel it is the only way to resolve what frustrates them.

They have one way of understanding it and one way to approach it: "Either I get what I want or I'm out of here!" Defuse this anger (after listening and being empathetic) by giving the person alternative ways to broaden how she perceives and approaches the upsetting experience. Rather than saying, "I can't do that for you," which sets a tone of finality and reinforces the angry belief that the person has to yell, because you will not help her, say, "I know it is frustrating and I'm sorry I can't do that for you, but let's talk about it and see what we can figure out." Or "I'm sorry we can't do that, but one thing we haven't tried yet to fix this is…"

Having alternative ways of approaching one's frustrating situation gives choices to the person. It makes her feel more in control which, if you remember, is what compels her to "stand up" in anger. Consider again Bonnie, who told Tom he could not get his medicine. Rather than blame him for being late or giving a simple "no can do" response, she could have listened and acknowledged his feelings and then suggested alternatives to resolving his situation. She could have said she would ensure the doctor saw him immediately the next morning or asked if he knew any other clinics she could call. This would have made Tom less agitated, because besides making him feel heard, he was given constructive ideas or plans that were beneficial to resolving what angered him. He would not think that the receptionist was trying to persuade him to do something that was not necessarily in his best interest and instead out of her own self interest, as if she were telling him what to do without concern for his welfare and rather because she wanted him to stop yelling at her. Tom instead would have been presented with choices that would have helped him take responsibility in doing something to help solve his problem. This responsibility would have made him feel more in control and less angry. It was this control and working on his problem, he would then realize, and not yelling that ultimately would resolve the situation that angered him.

Be careful if the irate person continues to be angry or expresses reluctance to work on the problem. He might be anxious attempting to resolve what angered him and so needs further support: "This is a tough situation and you are handling it well" or "It's good to see you trying to get a hold of this." It also makes the person less anxious knowing he is not alone in his attempt to resolve what angers him. "I know it's difficult, but we can deal with this" or "You might not think you can do it, but I am here to help you and together we will figure it out."

Another way to encourage a person to work on her problem is to invite her input. "What do you think we can do?" Get her engagement even when it is your idea. "Doesn't this make sense to you?" or "What do you think if we try this?" It also helps if you secure a verbal agreement. Ask for an "okay" at the end of what you say so the person feels she is giving input or agreement on the situation. If a person does not follow through on her agreement and returns to yelling, avoid the tendency to say, "I let you talk now let me talk." It will be met with, "What do you mean you let me talk? No one *lets* me talk; I talk when I want to talk!" Instead, remind the person of her agreement in order to get her back to resolving her frustration rather than shouting it.

Finally, help the person set in motion a concrete course to resolve the problem that angered him. "We seem to have figured it out; now what do we do to make it work?" Get the person to take the ideas and possible solutions you have discussed and turn them into a plan with definite tasks and specified deadlines. "Okay, so you will go right now to Social Security and talk to the supervisor—remember no yelling—about why you didn't get your check and what can be done to get it, right?"

If after all the listening and empathizing the person does not become calm and instead continues to scream or swear, then do not say, "I told you once and I'm not telling you again. Stop yelling!" This will escalate, not defuse, the yelling. Also do not in exasperation say, "*If* you really wanted to resolve this...." You will only get in response "What do you mean *if?*" Instead, patiently return to acknowledging the person's feelings and trying to get her to talk about what angered her rather than yelling about it. Anger is an intense emotion that does not disappear easily and several attempts might be necessary to defuse it. "I know you want to resolve this, so let's keep working at it until we do." If the anger continues unabated, then you are facing a more intractable and challenging stage.

TIPS FOR EFFECTIVE LISTENING

Here are some suggestions to achieve effective listening.

Do:
- Give attention to the angry person's problem
- Focus on what makes the person angry, not how he is expressing his anger
- Maintain good eye contact
- Use concerned facial expressions
- Sustain a sensitive tone of voice
- Acknowledge the person's anger
- Express empathy

Do not:
- Stifle feelings
- Order the person to stop yelling
- Roll eyes
- Frown
- Mumble
- Tap your fingers, look at your watch, etc.
- Interrupt
- Let your mind wander to think of other things

Successful active listening will help the angry person to talk about his problem rather than shout about it. Then you can begin problem solving with the angry person so he can resolve the issue that has made him angry.

CHAPTER 3

Defensive Anger

Some people do not stop screaming or swearing just because you listened to them. They might even do more: "Screw your support—just fix it!" You are now dealing with a major shift in anger's intensity. The person's yelling feels more than an expression of frustration and frequently seems out of proportion to what precipitated it. Mary's friends were always perplexed whenever she blew up over a seemingly small incident that, granted, might have been a bit embarrassing but certainly did not justify her angry outburst. They found themselves asking one another, "Why is she *so* angry?" or "We've done all we can to help her so why is she still yelling?"

Anger at this new stage expresses not only the frustration of being disrespected or ignored but also the emotional hurt that comes from it. This person yells not only because she does not get what she needs, but also because in not getting what she needs she was made to feel insignificant or inadequate. People like Mary never developed the confidence to directly manage mundane acts of adversity, such as being denied something, and instead feel rejected or belittled by them. They become angry as a result, because they learned it is preferable to yell about being ignored than to feel humiliated or like a failure from it. They do not feel powerless or hurt when they get angry. "I would rather be mad than sad" describes them.

Bart, the man we spoke about earlier, was angry at Social Security, because he did not receive his monthly benefit check. Social worker Robin's attentive listening would have calmed a person at the frustrated stage of anger, but not a person at this defensive stage of anger. This is because the denial of his benefits elicited a more intense anger than that derived solely from not getting a check. He was already embarrassed he needed Social Security and so when he reluctantly extended his hand for help and was denied, he felt belittled and humiliated. Bart always had trouble coping with feelings like these; they seemed overwhelming in his inability to "pull himself together" when he felt down or depressed. But he learned over time that anger made him feel less overwhelmed; that rather than feeling "pulled down" when emotionally hurt he could become angry and he did not feel emotionally wounded. He felt strong and in control when he yelled about not getting his check instead of feeling humiliated or controlled by the circumstances. He yelled so loudly, however, about not getting his check that it seemed out of proportion to what happened, especially when, as described earlier, Robin explained she could help and yet it didn't make any difference. Bart was *still* angry, because it was about not only being denied his check but also anger's ability to defend against anxiously feeling vulnerable and hurt due to that denial.

The social worker was unaware of her client's underlying defensiveness and, in turn, thought he was overreacting when he yelled about not getting his benefits. Robin believed he was "getting bent out of shape" over something that could be fixed. She became more strident in her attempt to constrain his anger, demanding adamantly that he stop yelling. He could not stop yelling, because it was the yelling that defended him against feeling hurt. To stop yelling would be to expose himself to feeling rejected or humiliated and so would intensify the hurt sense of pride he felt. To counterbalance this, he yelled more aggressively to defend against it happening.

Being yelled at or called names does not feel like a personal attack, as we will examine in later stages when it feels accusatory and even threatening. But it is definitely not an earlier stage venting of emotions. You feel the difference when anger is aimed directly at you. It has a force that makes you "back off", that lets you know to stop pursuing your present course and thereby refrain from being intrusive in the person's inner emotional vulnerability.

Let's return to the situation with Bart, who was angry at Social Security. Yelling was his way of defending himself against feeling vulnerable *and* against Social Security making him feel vulnerable. Whereas an earlier stage of anger had the man yelling in order to be heard about his missing check and even could lead to calming down once the Social Security representative listened, defensive anger is not so easily placated. It compensates for inner hurt feelings and is more aggressively expressed toward the Social Security worker, because it is the only way this person knows how to prevent others from making him feel hurt. The intensity of his words and the aggressiveness of his stance make it clear he not only wants his benefits but also will not allow anyone to make him feel unworthy of getting it. "Who are you to tell me that I don't get a check?"

Bart's anger at Social Security typifies how a person would "rather be mad" than experience the sad feelings he cannot manage. Being angry creates an emotional wall that protects the person not only against hurt feelings, but also against the one causing that hurt. Its intensity makes you not only ask yourself, "Why is she so angry?" but also "Why is she so angry at *me*?" Anger protects the person against feeling vulnerable *and*, in its aggressive reaction to you, defends against you making the person feel vulnerable. Anger's "standing up" to you makes the person bigger so as to not be ignored and also to more adamantly stop you from making her feel small—from feeling the vulnerability or hurt that comes from being ignored. It is his way of saying "you got too close", that you invaded his personal emotional space. You experience a greater intensity in an anger that is aimed at you, because the person is no longer shouting *about* her frustration and instead is yelling *at* you. She no longer swears *about* what happened but rather directly curses you. "Why are you being such a bitch?" is replaced with "You bitch!"

My friend Mike asked my advice on how to respond when his girlfriend Nicole became angry over seemingly insignificant incidences. She asked him for help on her computer, for example, and he said he was busy at the moment but would be available shortly. To this she yelled, "If you don't want to help me then never mind!" Mike wanted to help, but was momentarily occupied and so assumed his girlfriend should understand his response rather than yelling at him. Mike wanted to know if I thought Nicole was acting like a spoiled child or, more clinically, if she was compelled to get angry due to an immediate gratification orientation to life that made her irate when her needs were not instantly met.

I knew Nicole before their relationship and understood that her anger came from a deeper, more defensive need. She was a single parent with a young child and was concerned about their security. Living with my friend Mike made her feel secure, which was one of the reasons for moving in with him, but barely beneath the security was a fear that the relationship was not very solid—or at least not sufficiently solid to sustain its stresses—and that along with its shaky foundation was a shaky sense of security. So Nicole's defensively angry reaction to his not immediately responding to her request for help was, unbeknownst to him, not only about not getting her problem immediately fixed but also in response to the deeper insecurity she felt when any problem in their relationship elicited the fear that her security was superficial and at risk. If he could not help her with small things, she reasoned, how could she trust him with bigger issues, like being a reliable provider and making her feel secure? Failing to respond immediately to her request for computer help caused her to feel what it would be like if he failed to be available to take care of her, i.e., vulnerable and insecure. She never learned to directly manage or even acknowledge these distressing feelings and instead learned that anger made them disappear or at least not feel so overwhelming. So she yelled at Mike for not immediately fixing her computer.

Let us consider a man named Derrick who brought his wife, Susie, with him to counseling and whose presenting problem was that his wife's anger was damaging their relationship. Derrick said Susie became angry easily, as when he was late for something unimportant and she yelled at him for it. He often apologized and said he did not know it was important to her. Rather than accept his apologies, she always seemed to become angrier. "Why do you keep doing it? You know it drives me crazy!" Derrick sought counseling, because he wanted to learn why his wife became irate over seemingly innocuous events. He could not get Susie to help him understand her anger, as she became incensed whenever he tried to get her to talk about it. He also wanted to learn how to deal effectively with Susie's anger, which was causing a significant strain in their relationship.

Susie simply told her husband she was irritated by his tardiness. Derrick said he understood and took responsibility for it, but then asked why she became incensed when he tried to get her to talk about her anger so they could resolve it. She told him she was irritated by his insistence on talking about what angered her and would prefer that he simply apologize for it and commit to being punctual so as not to anger her again.

Derrick knew his wife would get angry in the future—whether it was due to his being late or another matter—so he continued telling her how important it was to discuss her feelings in order for them to more effectively deal with her anger—in spite of her warning that his insistence of talking about her anger made her angrier. This was too much for Susie, too much intrusion into uncomfortable feelings, which she warned him to stop doing. Eventually she blew up at Derrick and told him she could no longer take the way he made her feel. When asked to describe the feelings she was talking about, she at first refused or said it did not matter, but finally told him that his tardiness made her feel disrespected, as if she was unworthy of his being punctual. Susie acknowledged that the situations in which he was late might not have been very important, but his lack of concern for how his tardiness affected her made her feel she was unimportant and not special.

It was difficult for Susie to acknowledge these painful feelings—both to herself and to her husband—and so she became angry instead, because she found it easier. She did not know why she became angry; it was just something she learned to do when feeling upset. She became angry when he was late, because it made her feel poorly about herself and she became even angrier when he tried to get her to talk about why she was angry, because it felt like he was pushing her to talk about something that made her anxious.

Another person in a similar situation who could directly express these kinds of uncomfortable or painful feelings would be able to tell her husband that his tardiness upset her, because it made her think that he was irresponsible and that he did not care about how it made her feel. "I don't like it when you're late, because it says you don't care about me." He then could say he was sorry, that he did care about her and that he would be more diligent about being punctual.

Susie, however, who was in counseling with her husband, could not express her feelings directly and instead yelled at her husband for his tardiness and especially for his insistence on talking about these issues. Derrick did not know her anger expressed deeper defensive feelings and instead thought she was overreacting. He responded accordingly by asking why she was so angry and, when her anger was particularly intense, by more directly challenging the sanity of her anger, which made her more irate.

The cycle of escalating anger in this and other similar situations exhausted Derrick, eventually leading to his decision to no longer confront her anger. This choice seemed on the surface to be a good intervention since he learned by painful experience that confronting her anger simply made her angrier and he no longer could deal with her yelling at him. But choosing not to question Susie's anger did not defuse it and instead simply allowed Derrick temporarily to escape its verbal abusiveness. It was a passive response to anger. Susie's anger thereby successfully made him emotionally step back from intruding into her painful feelings, thereby keeping those unwelcome feelings suppressed.

Anyone involved in trying to defuse a defensively angry person, like Mike and Derrick with their partners, needs to recognize when anger is so protective of the person's hurt feelings that it causes you to emotionally stand back from the person. It does not make you physically stand back in fear, as we will see when it is hostile or intimidating, but it keeps you at a distance where you will not be able to further hurt the person's feelings, as was accomplished with Susie's increasingly intense anger and Derrick's withdrawal from where he could emotionally hurt her. Defusing defensive anger requires a correspondingly more elaborate intervention than when anger was simply to get you to be empathetic and listen.

Defuse Defensive Anger

Previously people were described as being angry at least in part as a way of defending against unmanageable feelings of vulnerability or insecurity. How do you curb a person's anger without making him feel vulnerable or insecure when it is this anger that protects him against these feeling? First you have to recognize the difference between anger that arises from frustration or being denied something and what defensively emerges from being emotionally hurt due to the denial. You do this by listening perceptively not only to what the person says but also how he says it. Some will protest, "But you earlier said not to address the *how* of a person's anger and instead *what* makes him angry." True and this is the major difference in defusing anger in the earlier stage of frustration and that of this more entrenched defensive anger stage. You listen to what angers the frustrated person and she stops yelling; you do the same with the defensively irate person and she continues to yell and maybe even gets louder. She is not pacified by your listening, because her anger is not only about your hearing what frustrates her but also is equally intent on guarding against hurt feelings as well as on adamantly making you know you cannot hurt her. You recognize in her yelling an intensity and persistence in spite of your listening.

Ben, a social worker I supervised, asked me to explain the difference between two people who came to him on separate occasions bitterly complaining about not getting food stamps. The first person he was able to calm by attentively listening, but when he expressed the same reassurance to the second person, she became even more aggravated. What Ben failed to observe was that the first person was relieved, because someone listened to her, which is what she needed even if (and especially if) in the end she did not get the food stamps. The second person was further angered, because the loss of food stamps made her feel an overwhelming vulnerability that she silenced *not* through someone's listening to her but by expressing the anger inside of her. Ben wanted the latter client's anger to be calmed in the same way the former client's anger was quelled. When it was not, he was at a loss as to why and what to do about it. Yet it was in the very intensity of the latter client's anger and in the client's resistance to being mollified that he should have identified the defensiveness of her anger and the need to intervene accordingly.

Let us return to the situation of the man who did not get his check from Social Security. Robin should have recognized a deeper anger than simply being denied a check when, in spite of saying she was sorry and she wanted to help—which would have been sufficient to defuse anger at the earlier frustration stage—Bart yelled louder rather than became calmer. Robin also should have noticed a more intense anger in the words he used to respond to her. If instead of shouting, "I cannot pay my rent," which would be an expression of his frustration, he shouted, "How dare you think you are not giving me my check", Robin should have recognized in Bart's anger something deeper than simply being denied a check. He was clearly letting her know not only that he was upset about not getting his check, but also that she had no right to make him feel upset and she needed to stop doing so. (And if he said something along the lines of "You had it in for me from the beginning" or "I'm not going to let you get away with this", Robin should have identified these as indicators that his anger belonged to more intense stages.)

What should you do when you recognize an intense anger that does not abate with listening and empathizing? First, stay calm. The defensively angry person can easily get "under your skin", especially considering that you have done your best to help her and yet she continues yelling. You might even be a bit angry yourself, because she is not simply yelling but yelling *at you* and you certainly do not deserve it. Telling yourself to stay calm helps you stay detached and not let the person's intense anger "push your buttons." It gives you the emotional space to remind yourself not to take her anger personally, that it is coming from a defensive need to protect herself from being hurt.

Jennifer, an oncology nurse, told me that one of the most difficult aspects of her job was dealing with angry teenagers whose cancer caused physical and emotional suffering that, at times, compelled them to scream at her for no significant reason. She knew the minor incidences that sometimes precipitated their yelling were a pretense, that they simply had to express their pain sometimes by yelling and that it was the only way at that moment to cope with feeling overwhelmed or to let her know that they did not want her to see them hurting, scared or needing help but they had grown weary of being sickly and so instead screamed their pain. This was especially true of the pain of wanting help and knowing that ultimately they were not going to get the help they needed, so it was preferable to scream that pain than to acknowledge it. Their anger was sometimes unbearable for the nurse—both the intensity of the yelling at her and the pain it represented. She often told herself to stay calm, to not take it personally and that it would pass by showing the patients the attentiveness they needed.

As we talked about in the section on early stage anger, do not order a person to stop expressing his anger. It is instinctual to want to protect yourself against a person's verbal abuse by demanding he cease yelling, but remember you are doing so with a person whose yelling defends against the anxious feelings that arise when made to feel vulnerable through acts such as your ordering him to stop being angry. The result is more yelling, not less. Jennifer knew this well.

Carl, a hotel guest who earlier in his life was momentarily caught in a hotel fire, was irate about having to leave his hotel room during a false fire alarm. He yelled loudly about the inconvenience it caused him. Of course his yelling was really a defense against emotionally re-experiencing the fear and vulnerability he felt in the earlier fire. He could not tolerate the sensation of helplessness that flooded him at the sound of the fire alarm and felt overwhelmed by it. Yelling about the inconvenience of the fire alarm distanced him from feeling vulnerable. Being angry felt safer than being scared.

This man's anger is not to be confused with a more intense rage we will examine in later stages that occurs when underlying feared feelings *do* overwhelm and erupt in out of control rage. The anger experienced at this stage defends the person against feelings that might be overwhelming. His yelling makes him feel in control. Cursing or shouting create a kind of a wall, an intense emotional wall behind which he maintains control of the vulnerability or hurt feelings he cannot directly manage and beyond which he keeps at a distance the interloper who threatens to penetrate this wall and expose these feelings. It adamantly tells you or whoever instigates the emotional pain that you are unwelcome behind that wall; that you are trespassing on forbidden emotional ground and need to step back.

Sarah, the building manager, told Carl, who was upset by the fire alarm, to stop yelling. She said other guests were also inconvenienced by the alarm and that his yelling had to stop, because it was interfering with her attempt to maintain calm in a stressful situation. Ordering Carl to stop yelling, however, exposed him to the anxious vulnerability he kept hidden beneath his yelling and behind his emotional wall, so he became even angrier in order to stand up to the manager's attempt to stifle his defensive yelling. At that juncture, Sarah should have recognized in his anger an intensity that suggested his yelling was not merely about the inconvenience of a false alarm. She would not know what it was that incensed him, but she would know it was not frustration or a personal attack against her. Rather than further demand that he silence his shouting, Sarah needed to intervene less forcefully and more incisively.

Think also of the earlier discussed Nicole and Susie, the girl-friend and wife who yelled at their partners for their inattentiveness or tardiness. Anger protected them against feeling hurt due to the men's insensitivities as well as pushed the men away so they could not further hurt them. When the partners did not heed the warning in the women's anger and instead confronted their anger and demanded they stop yelling, the women became incensed. Remember that their anger was an emotional wall that protected them both from unmanageable inner feelings and from their partners' probing intrusion into those feelings. When these men confronted their partners' anger, it felt to the women like the men were trying to breach that defensive wall. Nicole and Susie were not going to relinquish their anger simply because their partners expected it: Anger protected them from inner hurt feelings and from those making them experience it. They were not going to surrender that which protected them. The opposite happened. Their anger became more intense, not only as a defensive wall that protected them, but also a projectile that was aggressively hurled from behind the wall onto the interlopers so as to more forcefully push them back from getting too close to breaching the wall. This anger was no longer defensive in nature and instead had hardened into the hostility we will examine later. If instead these men had stepped back and validated the anger they evoked in these women, as we will discuss now, they would have defused that anger and restored calm.

Validate Defensive Anger

What should the hotel manager, husband or any of us in a situation with a defensively angry person do to defuse the defensive anger that makes a person resist calming down when becoming calm means abandoning the anger that critically protects them against underlying vulnerabilities? The answer is to listen *and* respond in a way that makes the person feel not only heard, but also less vulnerable and thereby less attached to the anger that defends against feeling vulnerable. This means validating the person's anger.

Validation is different from acknowledging a person's anger, which was discussed in the previous chapter. Acknowledging anger makes the frustrated person know not only you heard her anger, but also you understood what happened to make her this angry. The *defensively* angry person also cares about whether his frustration is heard but cares more about whether you hear he will not be made to feel hurt or vulnerable. Validating his feelings requires his knowing you are responding to something deeper in his anger than solely that of the external situation that frustrates him. You want him to know you hear he is angry because he was made to wait too long or was denied something but also that you understand he is more intensely angry because of how this makes him feel.

Remember Leo, the earlier stage angry person who was telling his friend Jason about being fired. If Jason was going to be able to help calm Leo down then it was important to acknowledge his anger before offering constructive insight (such as he should not have criticized his boss). At this defensive stage, however, the person's anger will not be mollified with empathy and a simple acknowledgement of what lead to the anger, which in Leo's case, was termination from his job. He wants to know that his friend feels why he is angry, that he actually "gets it." "That really sucks!" Letting the defensively angry person know you hear what angers him *and* you grasp how it affects him—"No wonder you are so angry"—defuses his yelling, because it was intended to convince you of how angry he is about the situation. But now that you validate his anger, he does not have to yell to convince you anymore.

Validating the person's defensive anger does not say you know the vulnerability or pain kept hidden beneath the anger. You cannot know the exact nature of these feelings: even the angry person does not necessarily know them. That is why he is angry: in part to keep hidden the hurt feelings he cannot directly manage. He thinks he is simply responding to a frustrating situation with a reasonable amount of anger (understandable since he is out of touch with what he really feels) when to everyone else it is obviously an inordinate amount of yelling or cursing.

If the defensively angry person candidly could acknowledge, "I'm afraid you won't help me and will make me feel more vulnerable and that is why I am angry," his anxiety would be made clear and you would understand his anger. But he cannot directly communicate his feelings and does his best not only to deny them but also to ensure you are not aware of them. You thereby experience intensity in his yelling but not the inner vulnerability or emotional pain against which his anger is a defense. Recognizing this intensity gives you the key to knowing a deeper defensive anger exists beneath the yelling *and* that in order to defuse the yelling you have to validate these underlying feelings without knowing exactly what they constitute. That is why Sarah, the hotel manager in the earlier described situation of the false fire alarm, not only had to resist ordering the anxious man to stop yelling but also had to validate what he was feeling, without in the process making him feel more of it. "I know this is lousy and I'm sorry for it, but I need to get everyone out of the building and I'd appreciate your help."

Similarly Derrick, whom we discussed earlier, should not have demanded that his wife Susie abate her anger nor should he have confronted her with its underlying pain—even if he knew what it was. Instead he needed to validate her anger. The intensity of its defensiveness should have alerted him to its message to stand back rather than push forward. Instead of demanding she stop being angry or trying to probe the anger's underlying urgency, he should have stepped back and let her know he understood her anger: "I'm sorry. I should not be late and it's not fair to you." The latter validates how she feels—disrespected, unappreciated—without directly stating it, but also acknowledging it is something deeper than the inconvenience of his tardiness. She feels more appreciated as a result and so too less angry since anger is no longer necessary to defend against feeling unappreciated.

Let us return to Robin, the Social Security worker who should have recognized a deeper anger in Bart, the man who did not get his benefit check. Robin would not exactly know the underlying hurt Bart felt, but she should have recognized that the intensity of his anger meant it was not just from not getting his check but also from how this situation made him feel. Then she would have known that confronting his anger would exacerbate it, because doing so would reinforce its function both to keep him from feeling humiliated and her from making him feel that way. Rather than saying, "I'm going to help you so stop making a mountain out of a mole hill," she should have let him know she would help him *while* making sure he knew she understood how he felt: "Sorry you didn't get your check. I can only imagine how it must make you feel. Let's figure out what we can do about it." Substitute the word *medicine* for *check* and the same could be said for the receptionist Bonnie and the client Tom, who was defensively angry due to feeling helpless when he could not get his medicine.

I am reminded of a similar albeit mundane situation which many of us have encountered, in which my friend Gina was unable to remove the cover off a jar. Seeing her struggle was fruitless, I took the jar and screwed off the cover. Expecting thanks or at minimum a joking "I got it loose for you," I instead got an irate, "Why did you do that? I just about got it off!" I was perplexed, because I was simply helping her and so responded, "Why are you angry at me? I was just helping." Gina was angry because she did not ask for help and wanted to get the cover off the jar on her own. On a deeper defensive level, however, she was embarrassed she could not do it herself and rather than acknowledge the embarrassment—or acknowledge the need for help that would also embarrass her—she became angry at me for doing it. To defuse her anger I had to validate how she felt without "rubbing her face in it": "You're right. Of course. Sorry."

Another common situation is when a person's boss reprimands him, such as in the case of Joe, and, being unable to deal with or even acknowledge the resulting feelings of humiliation, goes home and becomes angry over an unrelated although seemingly insignificant situation with his partner. Joe probably is not aware of the connection, but his anger at his partner Michelle is a defense against feeling the vulnerability he was made to feel at work but which he could neither express nor be angry about (for fear it could jeopardize his job, like Leo who was fired for criticizing his boss). The anger Joe experiences at home is not the earlier stage of venting frustration, which he would do by directly expressing his anger about his boss, and instead is the displacement of his anger at his boss with anger toward Michelle. In this way, he is able to express indirectly the anger he brought home with him and do so without acknowledging the humiliation against which that anger was an emotional defense. Michelle is at best confused with Joe's inexplicable anger. Its intensity and the way it made her feel, however, tells her she needs to address his anger in a way that does not exacerbate it and instead validates that something is wrong. She does not say, "Don't take out your frustration on me" and she instead validates his feelings: "Obviously something has you very upset and I don't think it's just this little incident; do you want to talk about it?" (Oftentimes, validating a person's defensive anger is not sufficient to defuse his feelings and he needs to be more directly told that his anger is inappropriate.)

Michelle did not know the incident at work that instigated Joe's agitation just as I did not know the feelings beneath Gina's anger over unscrewing the lid and Bonnie, Gayle and Robin, receptionist, manager and Social Security worker, did not know the exact nature of the underlying feelings that made the people in their lives angry. But they, and all of us dealing with defensively angry people, need to recognize the deeper defensive anger in the intensity of a person's yelling and validate that deeper anger. Only then will the person feel his yelling has been heard and stop it: not only because his problem has been addressed, but also *how* his problem made him feel has now been validated. A defensively angry person lets go of some of the anger that protects against feeling vulnerable. When you validate how his anger makes him feel it also makes him feel less vulnerable.

Validating underlying feelings does not mean, as mentioned a few pages earlier, that you know exactly what they are *and* does not mean you tell the person what they are even if you think you know. Saying, "That's lousy" is very different from saying, "That must make you feel worthless." The irate person wants to hear the former—it validates how she feels—while the latter would reinforce what she does not want to feel and what her anger is meant to conceal. Telling my friend Gina, for instance, that her anger from my unscrewing the lid was due to feeling humiliated and it really was not important or Michelle saying to Joe that he was agitated, because his boss made him feel vulnerable or the hotel manager telling Carl, "You're angry, because the fire alarm scares you" would simply further frighten or humiliate them, which, as said, is something they could not handle directly and would then make them angrier. "Who said it was important—you shouldn't have grabbed the jar!" "I can handle my boss!" "You think a false fire alarm is going to scare me?"

However, do not ignore a person's underlying defensive issue that might arise in the course of trying to calm him. Had Bart, the person angry at Social Security, said, "Being denied my check is bad enough, but I really hate the way it makes me feel," do not respond, "We can't deal with that." Especially do not say, "You need to get over it!" The person's underlying humiliation or vulnerability can be so overwhelming that it is more pressing than the problem itself or at least pressing enough that, if not adequately addressed, will remain an obstacle to defusing the situation. This is not the moment, however, for a therapeutic intervention—which you might neither have time for in an emotional crisis or the training to do—but neither is it something to dismiss. Validate what the person feels and let him know it should be discussed further. But, in another instance, what is important at that moment is helping him resolve the situation that angers him. "I can see why that (not getting medication or a check, for example) would upset you and we should definitely look into it. For now, though, let's work on solving this problem."

Set Limits to Anger
Validating a person's defensive anger might soothe the underlying anxiety that precipitated the yelling, but you must be careful not

to inadvertently instigate more yelling via validating his feelings. Telling the person, "I can see why you are angry", for example, might have made him think his anger was heard in the earlier frustration stage, but it can make the person at this defensive stage feel his more intense yelling is acceptable, that the aggressive yelling that kept you at a distance was warranted—even effective—and thereby feel encouraged to continue: "You can see I'm angry? Well then do something about it and do it now!"

Remember the earlier described hotel manager, Sarah, who ordered the defensively angry resident, Carl, to stop yelling during the false fire alarm. Had she realized that ordering him to stop screaming would be counter-productive and instead was inclined to tell Carl it was okay to yell, he might have interpreted her support as license to yell more. This would have been detrimental to the manager's maintaining control of the situation—including Carl's yelling—in order to facilitate everyone's safety. Sarah needed to validate Carl's anger, as described, so as to make him feel less vulnerable *and* at the same time she needed to let him know it was not acceptable to yell at her.

Reining in a person's anger and validating it requires a tricky mixture of setting limits to the person's *expression* of his anger while simultaneously being supportive of his feelings. The former—a reprimand for the inappropriateness of his yelling—without the latter support of his anger would result in the person feeling more vulnerable and angrier, while the support of how he feels without some constraints being placed over how loudly or forcefully he expresses it would result in unbounded and potentially explosive anger. Instead, what is required is the reining in of the person's aggressive behavior while not making her feel vulnerable or humiliated in the process. You want the person to know you are telling her to stop yelling because it is abusive, but you still grasp why she is angry. Rather than an open-ended, "Go ahead and yell; it's good for you" or a more confrontational, "You can't yell at me just because I'm late," either of which can escalate the person's anger, let the person know you understand she is upset *and* let her know she has to rein in how she expresses her anger: "Of course you're angry, but I need you to stop screaming at me." "It's okay to be angry, but it's not okay to yell at me."

What particularly works is that these kinds of statements, which validate a person's feelings while controlling the yelling, do not tell the person to *stop* being angry, only to temper the way he expresses it. This is a more realistic and attainable goal for the per- , son who defensively *has* to be angry and who is not likely to suddenly stifle his anger on command. Feeling supported and being asked to be patient or to lower one's voice does not feel like one is being pushed into an emotional all-or-nothing showdown: one in which the person is compelled either to continue yelling out of a defensive need to silence inner anxiety or to stop yelling and as a result anxiously feel vulnerable (thereby stimulating a return to being angry). Instead he can remain angry, as he needs to be to defend against inner hurt feelings, while quelling his boisterous tone. And doing so further dissipates his defensive anger, because it helps him recognize that what he thought was simply an angry standing up for himself really was louder or more aggressive than he realized. When Derrick told his wife he understood how his tardiness must have made her feel *and* asked if she could quiet her yelling so he could tell her how he was going to work at being more responsive to her needs, she felt her anger was validated while recognizing it no longer had to be strident. She responded by curtailing her screaming.

I supervised a worker named Bill who became irate in response to the slightest amount of constructive criticism. Whenever I said he was coming in late too often, he became defensive. He was upset with me, because in his mind I had no reason to belittle him, especially since he was doing a good job and he was having trouble in his home life. Of course I was not belittling him, but criticism of any kind made him feel humiliated. He became perturbed and testily gave excuses for whatever I said was not being done properly. This was his way of defending himself against feeling humiliated or rejected. It was also his way of trying to get me to ease up on my criticism so I would not get close to his vulnerability.

"You have no right to say this to me—I do a great job and you are complaining about my being a few minutes late!"

I initially confronted Bill's anger, letting him know it was inappropriate: "Stop making excuses and listen to what I'm telling you." This made him angrier, because it caused him to feel more vulnerable: "I'm not making excuses; you just don't want me to do my job!" I realized that if I continued to confront his increasingly intense anger, he would become overtly hostile. I learned not to confront his anger and, instead, to validate his feelings; to say I understood why he was upset and that yes he was doing a great job. This made him less defensive and bolstered his self-esteem around his work. I then could directly address his anger and his need to rein it in: "I know you are upset, because you are doing a good job and it feels like I am criticizing you, but I assure you I am not. If you could let go of some of that anger I think you will hear that I am just trying to make this work better for all of us."

Let's return to Robin, the previously discussed Social Security worker who recognized a deeper defensive anger in her client who did not get his benefit check. She needed to let him know that she understood how not getting a check must have made him feel *and* that he could not yell at her. "I realize this means a lot to you and I'm doing all I can to help, but I need you to stop yelling." This would make Bart think someone heard how it made him feel not to get a check, which is what he needed in order to respond less defensively to the request to stop yelling. The vulnerability he kept hidden beneath his yelling would remain cloaked even though he was told to stop yelling, because he was made to feel his anger was validated and thereby was not made to feel less vulnerable. (Do not be surprised that even if Bart gets his check that he probably will not leave the office without uttering a few more choice invectives about the way he was treated, as a way to defend against the emotional hurt he was made to endure and to convince others he was not hurt.)

Consider also the experience so many have had of being called some racial or gender epithet. You immediately (and understandably) want to respond, "Don't call me a [fill in the blank]!" This will not de-escalate the irate individual whose slur is a defense against inner hurt feelings and instead will incite him to yell back, "But you are a [fill in the blank]!" Instead, validate his feelings and simultaneously set limits to his expression of his feelings by saying, "I know you have good reason to be angry, but you wouldn't want someone calling you that so please don't say it to me."

As a final example, let us return to Bonnie's criticism of Tom when he was late for his doctor appointment. She should have recognized in Tom's highly charged emotional state that he did not comprehend her explanation that she could not get his medicine because the doctor was gone and that instead he heard an accusation that he was irresponsible, because he was late and he needed to stop yelling. Bonnie should have then responded in a way that did not make Tom feel criticized for being upset nor humiliated for the deeper feelings of vulnerability that made him angry while at the same time letting him know he needed to curb his verbal abuse: "I realize this means a lot to you and I'm doing all I can to help, but I need you to stop yelling so I can do it."

Tom felt personally attacked when the receptionist instead told him she would not tolerate his anger, which of course made him defensively angrier, to which Bonnie became defensive herself: "You're crazy for yelling at me when it is not my fault you are late!" Tom's response ratcheted up even more, because he felt she was trying to teach him a lesson by hurting him or was deriving perverse pleasure in denying his medicine. "You think this is crazy? I'll show you crazy..." What began as anger defensively expressed against being treated dismissively escalated into hostility and even violence, as we shall see in the next chapters. Before we get to that, however, we will take a brief look at a distinct expression of defensive anger that comes from the narcissistic personality.

Narcissistic Anger

You know what the narcissist is like: he is charismatic and gregarious, animated and self-assured, yet something about him makes you think these characteristics are superficial. You are further convinced of it when the person too quickly loses his charm and becomes angry over minor disagreements. That is because his charm and confidence are phony, comprising an inflated sense of importance and self-absorption that is a defense against underlying feelings of insecurity or vulnerability. The anger that erupts so easily is what protects him against these feelings, feelings which arise whenever someone challenges the self-importance that normally keeps them hidden.

Fred is an acquaintance with whom I engage in various athletic events and who is very charming with women players—almost seductively so—as well as with men. He is very competitive at sports, but no less witty and engaging; that is, unless, he loses a game. Then he uses his charm to be dismissive of the loss, as if it was of no consequence or to make fun of the event so as to take away any credibility from the loss. The discerning person, however, could recognize the disappointment barely concealed beneath the veneer of his being above it all. And when the defeat is too obvious a reflection of a poor performance to be dismissed as irrelevant, Fred becomes overtly angry. He smashes the ball on the ground or loudly exclaims various excuses for losing the match, such as blaming his teammate's incompetence. He is not mean, but clearly lets others know that the loss was not due to any inadequacies on his part.

Fred's anger is the result of narcissistically clinging to his projected image of being a superior athlete. Losing a match exposes to others and to himself the superficiality of that idealized image and, in the way he manages the loss, the insecurity hidden behind it. His charm disappears as he belittles the opponents or blames the teammates with whom he was moments earlier engaging in friendly banter. He cannot tolerate the loss and especially the vulnerability and insecurity it elicits, because he never learned to manage these feelings directly. He is supposed to win all events or at least be dignified about losing in a competitive match, but he does not know how to handle losses that are due to abject failure and cannot handle them with dignity. He instead learned anger would contemptuously dismiss the loss and, at the same time, demonstrate (to others and to himself) that he was not weak or inferior and instead was still above it all. Those who played with him learned not to challenge his outbursts, because they knew he would become angrier and they also knew that by the next time he played he would have abandoned his anger and would be back to his charming disposition.

It is difficult to prevent a narcissist from being angry. My athletic acquaintance inevitably became angry if he lost a game and there was nothing to be done to stop it. The narcissist possesses a persistent predisposition to anger when situations do not fulfill his inflated sense of importance. And this happens frequently due to his unrealistic expectation that you—whether you are a sports partner, friend or spouse or especially if you are in the helping professions—will unfailingly gratify his needs. When the latter does not happen, when you are slow in fulfilling his expectations or you deny something he needs, he becomes intensely angry to defend against the resulting insecurity or vulnerability he is made to feel.

The narcissist's anger defends not only against feeling vulnerable but also against you for making him feel this way. "I don't have to put up with this!" You expose a crack in the armor of self-importance when you do not live up to his expectations; his demeaning anger dethrones your idealized need-gratifying role in order to take back the power he invested in you to reinforce his importance. Saying, "You don't know what you are doing" erases the special image he endowed upon you and ensures he will not be hurt again by having expectations you will not fulfill. It also pushes you away with its intensity so as to keep you at a distance from what he really feels.

My friend Courtney was perplexed by the unexpected anger of a man she recently met. She felt "swept off her feet" by Mark and by his charm and seemingly selfless attentiveness. When after a relatively short time of dating he suggested they live together, she said it was too early for her. Mark affably said he understood and continued in his charming way to try to convince Courtney of how special she was and how special they were together, but she remained steadfast in her decision that it was premature to be living together. He then became angry, belittling her and even calling her stupid for not recognizing how great a couple they would be living together.

My friend could not understand Mark's anger. He was so charming and supportive and he already said he understood her reluctance to move in together, so why did he become irate when she refused his repeated suggestions that she should live with him? What she did not know was that Mark was accustomed to his charm and flattery seducing people to his way of thinking and when unsuccessful, as when she would not be persuaded to move in with him, he became angry to conceal his failure. Anger protected him against the narcissistic wound inflicted by her refusal to be charmed. He was not able to manage the rejection of his inflated self-image and, more dramatically, was not able to manage the sense of vulnerability it made him feel. Anger is what protected him from these feelings and defended him against her for exposing him to them. Anger also hurt Courtney's feelings, which was a way of getting back at her for hurting his feelings and also made her emotionally stand back from him where she could not further hurt him.

Courtney was so incredulous about her boyfriend's anger that she confronted him about it and he responded by becoming incensed. "How dare you criticize me—I'm only thinking of you and this is how you repay my kindness!" Similarly, telling the athlete he is a jerk for getting angry at his teammate about losing a game will inflate his anger, just as will happen with reprimanding the entitled person who loudly voices her displeasure at waiting in line like others. "Why do you think you are so important? There were people waiting here before you."

How should this woman have responded to her boyfriend's narcissistic anger? Similarly, how should you respond to an athlete who needs to win every game and becomes angry when he loses? What do you say to the person who becomes upset waiting in line because somehow she should not have to wait like others? How do you manage the entitled person who yells at you when you cannot give him what he expects?

The problem is that confronting narcissists' anger might make them angrier, but doing nothing about their anger or simply telling them everything "is okay" (in an attempt to temporarily heal the wounded self-image that exposed them to underlying insecurities about not being the perfect boyfriend/athlete/person who should not have to wait in lines like others) simply indulges and even exacerbates their narcissistic compulsion to belittle those who do not fulfill their needs and thereby raises their egos above those less deserving people. Being supportive of their anger helps the narcissist think it was acceptable to call his girlfriend stupid for making her own decisions or it was allowable for the athlete to be a jerk toward his teammate or it was the woman's right to be treated differently from others waiting in line.

The solution to de-escalating the angry narcissist, as described earlier in regard to de-escalating defensively angry people in general, is to be supportive of what makes the person angry and to set limits to how it is expressed. Let the person know you are attentive so she feels special and at the same time do not indulge her lofty image of self-importance. The difference between support and indulgence is critical. Indulgence is license to express anger in the abusive manner the narcissist feels defensively entitled to do when she feels hurt. Support, on the other hand, reinforces a person's self-esteem but does not bolster her bloated self-importance. You make her feel important as you should make anyone feel important who at that moment is instead feeling hurt or insignificant, but you do not indulge the exaggerated importance that makes her full of herself and think she is more important than others: expecting even more from you and being even angrier when not getting it.

You tell the athlete, for example, that he played a good game *and* that he does not have to be upset, because there will be another game where he can "show his stuff." Or the girlfriend tells her suitor she is flattered by his intentions, but he has no right to be angry with her if she is not ready to commit to the relationship. This simultaneously sets limits and provides support. You do this when you tell the narcissist who complains bitterly about waiting in line that you know her issues are very important and you need her to be patient so that you can help her as soon as you finish the present situation.

You also need to set limits for a person to whom you are providing support but cannot help due to a particular regulation. She in response might narcissistically proclaim, "Those rules don't apply to me!" Do not agree with her—which would indulge the bloated self-image that she is above normative constraints others have to follow—but also do not make her feel unimportant by saying, "The rules *do* apply to you!" Remember, anger is a defense for the narcissist and you do not want to strip her self-importance, because it will leave her exposed to overwhelming inner feelings. Instead, make her feel important so she does not feel insecure while at the same time setting limits: "I know this is important to you and that is why I need you to stop yelling so I can try to help."

These interventions give the narcissist the respect she needs to feel important and at the same time let her know the same respect is expected from her. My own original attempt at implementing these interventions was challenging because of my own issues in regard to how the angry narcissist's sense of entitlement "pushes my buttons." A demand such as, "You're getting paid to help me so help me" made me want to confront this person and even expose the insecurity beneath her imperiousness. Eventually recognizing how my own issues were impeding my ability to effectively de-escalate a narcissistic person's anger, I disciplined myself to stay detached from the person's obvious provocations and learned to agree with her that I *was* there to help her *and* that she needed to stop yelling so I could do my job. This made the person feel important and set limits to her abusive anger. Further, it established the limitations that I was not the idealized person she expected to fulfill her needs and that she could not abuse me for this, which she could accept with less anger because I made her feel important even as I set those limits.

A note of caution: A narcissist's charm can flatter you into believing you are the best worker or friend he ever had. The result can be a subtle seduction into allowing or even encouraging the narcissist's idealization of you: it feels good to be appreciated. It also feels good not to have to deal with the narcissist's demeaning anger—the result of your approaching his anger via the heights of the idealized image he bestowed on you that inspires you to do your best to gratify his narcissistic needs—rather than directly help him learn how to calm his anger (some of it uncomfortably aimed at you) and cope with the realistic limitations you placed upon it. Remember that you will be faced with even more intense anger when ultimately you cannot gratify one or more of his more intractable needs; you will have a greater height from which to fall when his resulting anger more aggressively pushes you off your idealized pedestal: "I thought I could count on you but you are no better then the rest of them!"

KNOW YOUR LIMITS

- Defensively angry people need you to validate their anger so they know their frustrations have been heard and that you will not make them feel vulnerable. Reflect on times when you were made to feel defensive or vulnerable. Compile a list of things you can say to validate another person's anger in order to prevent his feelings of vulnerability from intensifying.

- Setting limits on a how a person expresses his anger is crucial for you to defuse his anger and help him regain control of his emotions. What are the boundaries of a person expressing anger with which you feel comfortable?

- Know your limits of handling another person's expression of anger before getting in a situation with an angry person. This way you can set limits for the angry person without having to take the time to think about appropriate bounds.

CHAPTER 4

Difficult Angry People

A challenging group of angry individuals that we normally do not think of as being defensive are those we generally call difficult people. They are chronically argumentative, abrasive, opinionated and obstinate. They might not yell at you, but their anger is discernable beneath the criticism, sarcasm, contentiousness and contrariness: you ask them to sit and they stand or you ask them to do one thing and they'll do another.

Psychiatry refers to some of these people as having an oppositional defiant disorder. They are non-compliant, disrespectful of authority and deliberately annoying. They have a negative attitude toward you and possess unrealistic demands so you can never fulfill what they ask. In this way, they will always have something about which to complain.

Being difficult generally is a means of "standing up to you" in order to keep you at an emotional distance. The person's uncooperative ways establish an imposing if not impossible relationship with you, which is preferable to one in which you inevitably will deny or disappoint her, as is her deeper fear.

Deliberately being demanding is a means to test your limits in order to find out if you are good enough to deal with the person's problem. It is better defensively to argue with you, to criticize your supposed incompetence, to challenge you, to thwart your efforts than it is to calmly interact with you only to have you in the end not come through for the person and hence make him feel the rage or hostility—as we will examine in later stages—that comes from being rejected or emotionally hurt.

The difficult person's anger is typically less emotional than that of the frustrated person's. Rather than yelling or swearing, for instance, it is more goal-oriented: the person uses anger to push his argument on you, to wear you down, to make you feel guilty or doubt yourself with constant criticisms. "She's actually a very nice person, so maybe there is something in what she is saying." Or she might find fault in your work or words and then harp on it, trying to embarrass you in the process. "If you knew what you were doing I would not be in this situation now!"

The disagreeable person excels at expressing her anger indirectly through classic passive/aggressive behavior. She will be uncooperative rather than directly letting you know she is angry. If you ask a question as to why she is angry, she will ignore you or defiantly not answer. She might not say anything, but her silence is filled with anger. If she answers, she will not give a straight answer or will be evasive, especially if your question potentially reveals a truth she does not want to validate. She may answer your question with a question or with a monosyllabic response. And if you challenge her—"Why are you being so argumentative?"—she will respond, "Oh, so you don't want me to talk" and will be silent in order to passive/aggressively frustrate you.

Claire, a woman with whom I was doing couple's counseling, was trying to understand her husband Andy's obstinacy. She was frustrated to the point of leaving him, which, over the duration of the counseling sessions, she began to realize, was the motivation behind his stubborn ways. He was content in their relationship, even loving, but for some reason unknown to Claire, he at times became adamantly uncooperative. He would not do what she asked, even involving simple requests, and either ignored her or offered some absurd reason for not doing what was asked of him. For instance, Claire asked Andy to help her turn off the stove gas valve and he said he was too busy. When she said it was important because it was dangerous to leave on, he still refused, telling her it was necessary that she learn to do it on her own so she would not rely on him. Claire told him that was crazy, that she needed his help and then insisted on knowing why he would not provide it. Andy responded by becoming more obstinate and overtly angry. Over the lengthy course of our talking about issues like this one, Claire gradually learned from her husband that he was afraid she was going to leave him. He felt he was not as smart or sophisticated as she was and rather than demonstrate his incompetence when she asked for assistance and thereby give her reason to respect him less, he pushed her away—even to the point of her contemplating divorce—by not cooperating with her. It was better that he keep her at an emotional distance with his obstinacy than she reject him for being at best incompetent and, at worst, unworthy of her love.

The difficult person, like this husband, does not respond positively to persistently being questioned as to why he is being uncooperative. He will not suddenly become cooperative in response to your inquiries and instead will continue to be unhelpful. He will probably become more steadfastly difficult, such as responding sarcastically or critically, so as to more defiantly deflect the truth of why he is being difficult. He will be intentionally confusing, telling lies and not giving facts or twisting them so as to prevent any reasonable discussions. His response is not irrational, however, as with the schizophrenic or the person who is so intensely angry she does not think rationally. You can reason with a difficult person, but it will be frustrating, because he will be purposefully disruptive or disagreeable so as to create an unstable interaction that can make you feel less in control and thereby make him feel more in control.

Consider the working style of Zack, a clinical social worker I supervised. He was never mean or defiant, but he always had to complain about his tasks. It was always that his clients were too demanding, his responsibilities were unreasonable or a particular goal was unrealistic. I attempted to address his issues, trying to put them in a more benign perspective or to help him see how he could approach them differently and more effectively, but either he disagreed with or accepted what I had to offer and then found something else about which to complain.

I eventually recognized a pattern to his difficult behavior. Zack did a good job even though he complained about it, always timely in his responsibilities and effective in what he did. I noticed, however, that when he had nothing about which to complain—maybe because a particular task was completed or I had acquiesced to his grumbling and adjusted his assignment—that he became anxious and agitated until he found a new reason to complain. The complaining helped him once again to become focused and efficient. Griping about whatever he did gave him the energy to be productive and helped him feel in control of his work, while also silencing an inner anxiety that revealed itself when he was not complaining.

Rather than complain, a difficult person may constantly correct you. From her mindset, her perspective is always right and she will not tolerate the possibility that your perspective can also be accurate. At best, she ignores your ideas and, when she does react to them, she is contentious or critical. Or she will "one up" you whereby whatever you say she has something better to offer—something that challenges your ideas—demonstrating she knows more than you. As a result, you feel as though whatever you do is not right for her and often you find yourself having to defend yourself or doing something against your better judgment in order to mollify the person. And if, out of exasperation, you demand she stop arguing, she will probably say with a smirk (knowing she "got to you"), "Why are you so upset? I was just kidding."

Particularly challenging is that the difficult person not only corrects you but also keeps arguing with you until he gets what he wants. He turns everything you say into a contest and then needs to win that contest by proving you wrong or inept. To this end he dominates your conversation, does all the talking, allows you little to say in the matter and interrupts or contradicts what you say, at the cost of any valuable insight you might have to offer. He would rather keep arguing than to accede to your having the upper hand in providing a solution.

Aaron, an acquaintance in one of my social circles, always had to correct people. It was almost a compulsion, a need to interject his disappointment over someone misrepresenting the smallest issue or to illuminate others to a fact that only he knew. It did not matter that his interjection was annoying, which probably was apparent to him, even if others disagreed with him and presented facts contrary to his position, Aaron insisted on his correctness. It was important to him that others knew he was seemingly smarter than them. It might annoy them, but it was more important then their potentially thinking he was not as intelligent as them, which would have made him feel intolerably insecure.

This constant competition puts the difficult person in control and that is important to him. Being in control makes him the winner and, in his mind, makes you the loser. He is the winner *even* if he does not get what he wants. First, being difficult frustrates you and frustrating you becomes as important as dealing with the issue that upsets him. Second, he wins because he keeps arguing and as long as he is arguing, he is in control and he has not accepted defeat. This maintains an illusion of victory. The danger of this ongoing argument is that unabated anger builds in intensity until, as sometimes happens, the person has had enough of the arguing and becomes hostile, when up to that point he was just being difficult and argumentative.

I knew a supervisor, Jared, of a social service program who exemplified the need to be in control via being deliberately uncooperative with his staff. He was not a mean man, nor someone acting out of being frustrated. He simply was difficult, as when he did not make the workers' job assignments clear, refused to help with their tasks when they asked him questions or did not give good guidance. Being uncooperative made him feel in control, because his workers would never clearly understand their tasks and this would make them, first, rely on his authority to accomplish goals and, second, never fully succeed in their tasks and would not pose a threat to his being the expert.

Disengage the Difficult Person's Contest

The first task in working with the difficult person is to be careful, though not because of a danger of violence. Be careful, because the difficult person has a unique knack to pull you unaware into her anger. She possesses an uncommon ability to "get to you." Maybe she learned earlier in life that she had to be difficult and demanding in order to get attention—even negative attention is still attention—and subsequently learned to "read" people so as to know where they are vulnerable. She knows how to "get to you" whether by challenging everything you do or by arguing with anything you suggest. She does this *because* she wants you to argue or engage in a contest of wills with her, which gives her reason to be more obstinate or competitive.

Arguing with the difficult person means she has successfully "gotten to you." You might think you are only refuting her contentious ways, but in reality she has successfully drawn you into her emotional drama or into the power struggle to see who is in charge and who has the last word. Without even being aware of it, you suddenly find yourself compelled to win rather than cooperate with her to resolve the conflict. Your interaction descends into a cycle of defending yourself when everything you do is criticized or contested and you become more defensive until eventually you find yourself losing sight of your objective (defusing anger) and feeling lost in a contest over who wins the argument. That is where I found myself with Zack, the worker who always argued about his assignment or complained about his job, which eventually "got to me" and dragged me into a constant contest about who was the one in charge.

Remember this: you will not win a contest with someone who is compelled to be difficult. She has a *need* to be right and so anything you say, no matter how helpful, will be argued rather than heard. Whatever you suggest will become a debate of who is right and who is wrong and because she thinks she knows more than you and that she has to prove herself right and you wrong, she will not quit the argument until she wins (or at least will contentiously prolong the argument, which is also a form of winning).

You will be tempted to argue with the difficult person or correct him of his misperception that you are incorrect. The result will be an increasingly heated debate rather than de-escalation. "You are wrong!" "No, *you* are wrong!" The person might even add defamation to his accusation. "And you're crazy to think you're not wrong!" He adds the latter not only because he wants to argue but also because name-calling is his way to make the argument more personal and thereby draw you into his emotional drama. It "pushes your buttons" and you find yourself arguing with him, eventually becoming frustrated and finally, out of exasperation, either defensively blurting out, "Look what you made me do" or giving up and acquiescing to his demands.

You do not want to argue with the difficult person nor do you want to take her verbal abuse or disrespect, as discussed in previous chapters. The challenge at this stage of anger is that it is not as easy to stay detached from a person's verbal abuse as when you knew it was not personal or it came from frustration. You now take it personally, because you know the person's contentiousness is a deliberate attempt to "get to you." You become determined to prove you are in authority, not her; that you are right and she is wrong. Your motivation is not about defusing her anger: it is about power. It is about who controls the conversation, who will back down first or who has the last word. Even though it might defuse the person's anger if you let her feel in control or let her have the last word, you are emotionally invested in winning the power struggle. In the end, however, you will have an angrier person and you will have lost the contest if for no other reason than you engaged in it. That is why I never "won" the argument I had with my obstinate worker Zack. He never relinquished the contest, even surreptitiously sabotaging my supervisor role, and even if I was able to rein in his contentiousness I was embarrassed—and he knew as a result that he had won a victory—due to even engaging in a contest with him.

Reconsider Gayle, the manager I described earlier who engaged a client in a shouting match. I intervened when I saw the argument escalating, asking the client as a favor to stop the arguing. He complied but had to "save face" by getting in the last word: "Okay, but she can't talk to me that way." That should have been the end to this verbal contest, with a sense of success in having defused a heightening volatile situation. It required validating the difficult person and allowing him to have the last word, the last dig at the manager, which he needed for his own pride, especially considering he had already swallowed his pride in acquiescing to my asking him to stop arguing.

The problem was that Gayle's pride was also engaged in the argument, such that even though the difficult person was now calm and the crisis averted, *she* had to get in the last word: "Yeah, well, I am a manager here and you shouldn't talk to me that way." But the client did talk to Gayle that way and in response to her challenge, he would now talk to her more intensely that way. Anger that escalates in intensity—whether from frustration into defensiveness or hostility into rage—becomes more unwieldy, volatile and potentially dangerous. The primary goal of de-escalating anger is to defuse it before it becomes too intensely unwieldy or volatile to de-escalate. If this meant the manager should have "swallowed her pride" and reined in her tendency to correct the angry client then that is what she should have done. It would have helped restore calm and avert an escalating crisis.

The manager, however, did not resist the urge to respond critically, which rekindled their argument by making the difficult person feel his face was being "rubbed" in his acquiescence. The contest was again on and turned into more intense mud-slinging: "What are you talking about? You're the one who stuck your ugly nose in my business!"

Gayle was drawn into engaging the earlier described *how* of the person's anger. She lost focus on what made him angry and became stuck in the arguing and contentiousness. The result is that what began as an argument inflated into hostility. You do not want to ignore *how* the difficult person expresses his anger, because it can be disruptive. You want to help him calm *how* he expresses his anger—his criticism or arguing—but you want to do so without being pulled into its drama and thereby losing focus on dealing with the problem itself.

Defuse Difficult Anger

De-escalating the difficult person's anger begins with not getting dragged into it. It is challenging, of course, to not argue or get pulled into a person's anger when everything you say is thrown back at you as being incompetent or everything you do is rejected. You might be tempted to give up trying to help the difficult person, because in spite of everything you have done to help he continues to be difficult. "He doesn't want my help so screw him!" Do not give up and do not engage in the person's power struggle. Do not let him goad you into "telling him off" when you know that is what you feel like doing and you know it is what he wants you to do. Tell yourself that although he wants to pull you into his drama you will resist it, that you are in control of what decisions you make and not him and that you are better than allowing yourself to be seduced into a contest of wills or to be dragged into an entrenched drama.

Heather, the store clerk who told me about how she responded to the angry customer who was having a bad day, also told me about customers who were not frustrated but who simply were difficult. They were not mean, but they were sarcastic, uncooperative, made her "jump through hoops" to get what they wanted and in the end changed their minds and asked for something else. Heather knew she could not confront them about their difficult ways, because they would become even more difficult and so she learned to stay detached, to let them be excessively picky. She waited until they finished their "little game of toying with me" and then told them that when they were ready she would help them and thereby did not engage in their challenging ways.

Do not, like the store clerk learned, insist on winning an argument with a quarrelsome person. Trying to make her agree with you or stop being contentious makes you come across as approaching her with a win/lose mentality: you win and she loses. "You will not get what you want if you keep arguing with me!" The person feels even more compelled to keep arguing or being defiant, because backing down is losing and losing means forfeiting control and being emotionally hurt. She thereby continues to be contrary or disruptive with the determination to make you eventually capitulate or at least to keep you in the contest, which makes her feel she has not lost. That is why my earlier discussed friends learned not to argue with Aaron, who always had to make himself appear smarter than they were. They knew he would not relinquish the right to be correct and so debating or even discussing his particular obsession of the moment was fruitless.

A win/win mentality, on the other hand, helps the difficult person feel you are not trying to make her lose in a contest of wills. Instead, it creates the impression you are approaching her in a way she can win even as you constrain her contentiousness. "Okay, I see what you are suggesting so let's not argue about it anymore." Saying something like this would silence the acquaintance who argued interminably if you engaged him in it.

What if the person continues to be contentious? "You see what I'm saying, but you've done nothing about it!" You will probably feel exasperated and as a result again find yourself being drawn into arguing with her: "I am trying to do something, but you keep being difficult." Do not do this, for it is what she expects and what motivates her. Instead of engaging in a contest with Zack, my worker who constantly grumbled over his tasks—"Would you stop complaining about how bored you are with you work and just do your job?"—which would provoke more grumbling from him—"I would if you gave me more challenging assignments"—I let him know I understood that work at times was tedious and rather than getting bogged down in its tedium I asked what suggestions he had to make it better. This helped me stay out of his emotional drama and maintain a win/win approach. "Arguing about what needs to get done is not getting us anywhere and not getting you what you want. So let's stop arguing and figure out what to do."

Acknowledge a stalemate if you reach an impasse with the difficult person (a "you are wrong"/"no, you are wrong" scenario) and address the issue supportively rather than negatively or sarcastically. "I'm listening to the way we are talking and realize we are not getting anywhere, so let's try again without arguing." Maybe the person continues disagreeing with you, so say to her, "I've tried everything I know, so please tell me how I can help you." This is certainly accommodating rather than confrontational, but what if she throws it back at you: "I don't know; you're the one who is supposed to be the know-it-all." Do not be goaded into this contest, arguing about who is right or competing to see who has more authority or who will back down first. Instead, try to work with her contentiousness in a way that lets her win while you maintain control.

When, for example, the uncooperative person rejects or negates everything you say ("Nothing you say works"), rather than respond to her positively ("Yes it does"), which will make the conversation go back and forth, validate why the person thinks it will not work. If you *agree* she has a point or even agree with part of what she says, she will be less inclined to defiantly push her position with you. You then can move the conversation to the acceptable boundaries of working on her problem. "There is something in what you say, but let's think of how we can work at this together instead of in opposite corners." This response does not come across as criticizing or competing with the person and rather as giving her motivation to stop being resistant to working with you. You will deflate her compulsion to compete with you when, against all expectations, she finds she is not in a contest with you.

Think again of Andy, the husband who was not cooperative with his wife Claire when she asked for help concerning mundane issues and who became even more obstinate when she confronted him about it. She could not win that contest since he was compelled to be uncooperative. Eventually, she learned not to confront him and instead assertively let him know she did not understand why he would not help her while at the same time not arguing with him about it. When Claire applied this strategy, Andy did not feel a contest with her and thereby relaxed his compulsion to be contentious.

Staying out of a person's contest, however, does not mean ignoring his verbal abuse. Without taking it personally or engaging in an argument, let the individual know his contentiousness or name-calling—"You're an idiot to think this will work"—is inappropriate. "There is no reason to talk to me that way." This will probably not end his contrariness since emotional defenses are behind it, so be ready for the retort that comes from a need to keep provoking you. "But you are an idiot; you've done nothing for me!" This person's compulsion to frustrate or argue with you means you need to directly address his provocations, otherwise they will continue. But do so in a non-argumentative style in order not to get drawn into a contest. You might say, "Do you want to keep calling me an idiot? Or can we work on the problem," hoping this will refocus his attention to resolving the problem rather than arguing about it. He might be more motivated by arguing and so flippantly answer, "Keep calling you an idiot!" Again, parry his provocation instead of engaging it: "Okay, you have made your point. Let's now figure out what to do about the problem."

You might have to more directly confront the person if he continues to be contentious. "I want to work on your problem and not argue with you about it, so let's stop the name calling and tell me what I can do to help." You should "win" in this interaction, because you did not succumb to his provocation nor escalate it; he also wins, because in spite of not engaging you in an argument, he did not back down from his position and at least is able to begin working on it.

Think of a person who defiantly puts his feet on your desk and you ask him to take his feet down and he says, "Why?" or "It's not hurting anyone!" He is defiant not to be hostile, but to be difficult, to engage you in a contest to see who will capitulate. You can get in a confrontation with him, demanding he remove his feet from the desk, but what are you going to do when he does not comply? Argue with him about it? Knock them off the desk? Call the police, because he has his feet on your desk? He is going to win and you are going to lose. Or you can let it slide, because you know a confrontation will result in an escalated situation. Letting it slide, however, might embolden him, so now he kicks the desk, demanding you help him. You neither want to acquiesce to his defiance nor argue with him about it. You instead want to address his behavior in a way that lets him know you will not be pulled into his drama and does not give him license to act it out. "Come on, you don't have to put your feet on the desk to get me to help. Why don't you take them off and tell me what I can do?" This takes away the contest and de-escalates some of his defiance, resulting in his slowly (to show he is in control) removing his feet from your desk.

Another typical behavior that is annoying and often leads to an argument is the person's compulsion to interrupt everything you say. You know his interruptions are not intended to be constructive and instead are simply to be difficult. But you also know that to rebuff his interruption and demand he let you talk will exacerbate the interruptions and cause arguing. "Stop interrupting me" results in "But you're not saying anything important!" Instead say, "I want to help you, but when you keep interrupting it prevents me from letting you know how we can fix your problem." This statement does not criticize the person's behavior and instead provides the support that encourages her to become responsible for whether her situation will be resolved.

You take the anger and contentiousness out of the difficult person by taking your ego out of the interaction and turning its direction away from a test of wills or a win/lose situation. The difficult person expects and is geared for a contest, but you defuse this determination when you do not engage in it nor let him pull you into his drama. It is challenging to be difficult with someone who does not argue with you, who tries to work together rather than competitively. The earlier discussed manager, Gayle, who told the client to stop arguing with her should not have become engaged in an escalating contest with him and instead should have let him have the last word, which would have allowed him to feel in control. At that moment this was more important than asserting her authority should have been. Gayle should have seen the client was more committed to arguing with her (in order to save face) than to resolving the situation that angered him. Rather than rebuff his difficult way she simply should have said, "We're getting nowhere arguing about this, so why don't we just stop and start again."

If in the end none of this works, if the person not only continues to be difficult but also becomes angrier and hostile, you are dealing with a more escalated stage of anger.

KEEP YOUR ANGER IN CHECK

Difficult people use their anger to stand up to you and get something they want. They can easily draw you into their anger without your realizing. Be prepared for when a difficult person to tries to increase your anger:

- Think of some techniques that will help you remain in the now and focused on the present situation.
- Review your personal list of anger warning signs and remain aware of them.
- Plan some statements you can think to yourself to help keep you calm, e.g., *He is trying to upset me, but I know how to handle it. This is a good time to take a few deep breaths of relaxation. I'm not going to let him push me around, but I'm not going to lose my control either.*
- Practice your physical relaxation exercises on a regular basis (e.g., slowing your breath, tensing and releasing your muscles) so you begin any confrontation with as little tension in your body as possible and so the techniques come to you naturally while defusing an angry person.

CHAPTER 5

Hostility

The fourth stage of anger marks a significant shift away from aggressive behavior being an expression of frustration or defensiveness to being an intense expression of hostility. Anger at earlier stages was a strong emotion that energized a person not to be helpless and instead to stand up for herself. But a person becomes angrier when standing up for herself results in feeling more ignored or helpless, not less. Some people resign themselves to these anxious feelings or run from them (this is the *flight* half of the fight/flight response we discussed in Chapter 1), in which case they are of little trouble to you, at least for the moment (flight can suddenly stop and turn around to become fight.) Others dig deeper into their fight response, dredging up more intense anger while physically activating larger amounts of adrenaline, all combining to make them confront you more aggressively to get what they want. They become hostile, intimidating and mean.

Anger that is aggressively aimed at you is what distinguishes this fourth stage. It is no longer the act of standing up for oneself or even of standing up *to* you and instead is a more aggressive act of standing up *against* you. The person is less angry *about* something and rather is angry *at* you. She curses you not for what you *do*—"You are a jerk for not getting me my voucher"—and instead as a verbal attack for *who you are*: "You incompetent jerk!"

Remember the manager, Gayle, who was in the spiraling shouting match with a client and who, in spite of my having defused the situation, still had to have the last word: "It's good we're not arguing anymore, but you should not talk to a manager that way." The client snapped back, "Keep your nose out of my business." Gayle inferred that he was referring to her large nose and so told the client to stop being disrespectful about her nose, at which point the client's response became hostile and personal: "I can't help it if you have a kike nose—just keep it out of my business!"

Hostility takes what was once a healthy *expression* of anger and turns it into a verbal *attack*. Yelling no longer is meant to get you to listen but to *make* you listen; being argumentative escalates into bullying; cursing is less about convincing you of something's importance and more about coercing you; a demanding demeanor turns into a general attitude of antagonism; an anger that "gets under your skin" now is more likely to "make your skin crawl"; standing up to you no longer is simply to let you know you cannot "walk all over me" or "push me around" and now is aggressively to "get in your face" or push *you* around.

Pushing you around in a hostile manner is not yet physical or a threat of violence. This does not mean it is not dangerous, though. It might not cause physical pain, but intimidation certainly can cause emotional pain. And the latter can lead to physical harm when not effectively de-escalated, as described in headline stories of youths who were bullied on the Internet and were not physically abused but whose psychological abuse resulted in physical retaliation or killing themselves.

Anger at this stage is pernicious and can leave emotional scars not only because it is expressed directly against you but also due to it possessing a malicious or even menacing quality. Most of us have known people who try to intimidate or bully others into doing what they want and who do not care if those people feel frightened or coerced as long as they get those people to do what they pressure them to do. This type of person slams a book down on the table to forcefully persuade you to do what he demands; giving you a queasy sensation, because you know it is meant to scare you. It is not the slamming of a book or the racist slur that in previous stages was meant to get your attention or to vent one's pent-up emotions. It is a vicious verbal assault that aims to intimidate you into doing something you normally would not consider.

Hostility is also not the defensive anger that protects the angry person against feeling vulnerable by erecting an emotional wall of anger that prevents you from getting too close. Instead, it is almost as if that angry wall was not effective in keeping you at a distance, as if you were still trying to breach its emotional barricade in spite of the angry warnings to desist, and so the person hurls projectiles of viciousness or belligerent bombast that is meant to aggressively push you back from the wall.

Remember our earlier examination of the husband, Derrick, who could not understand why his wife, Susie, became angry at him for being late until he learned it made her feel unappreciated and she defended herself against the resulting unmanageable vulnerability by becoming angry. Susie's anger was, in fact, an emotional wall erected to prevent him from making her feel vulnerable. When Derrick did not heed the warnings of her anger not to trespass in an emotional area that was off limits to him and instead confronted her about her anger, she felt as if he was trying to breach that wall and intrusively push his way into her vulnerability. She became hostile, cruelly attacking him so as to *force* him away from her hidden feelings. "Are you that stupid? Can't you see I hate you for bringing up this stuff?"

Remember also the earlier examination of Tom, who felt frustrated or defensively humiliated because he was told by the receptionist, Bonnie, that he was too late for his appointment to get his medicine. Tom yelled at Bonnie to get her to listen and, when he still did not get his medicine, yelled louder and more viciously to *make* her listen. He called her incompetent and uncaring no longer to merely compensate for his own feelings of humiliation, but rather to humiliate her. The smaller he made her feel—and she even appeared smaller, as if shrinking in fear—the bigger he felt and the easier it was to intimidate her to get what he wanted.

What makes hostility particularly pernicious is the blame behind it. The receptionist *deserved* Tom's meanness for what he felt she did to him. He might not think she did it purposefully to hurt him, but in his mind she could have resolved the situation if she wanted and so is responsible. He wanted her to feel hurt just as she hurt him. His anger became less directed at what upset him and more directed at the receptionist for standing in the way of resolving what upset him. "It's your fault that I'm not getting my medicine!" Assigning blame makes the person feel he has the right to be angry at the accused person and renders him more resistant to being calmed. "Stop yelling at you? You're the reason I'm yelling!"

Think of the example of accidentally bumping into a person whose anger is mollified when you apologize. The hostile person *blames* you for bumping him and as a result, aims his anger directly at you: "Watch where you're going!" He does not accuse you of bumping him intentionally, but his belligerence makes it clear he wants you to know it's your fault and that he will not be so easily calmed with your apology. "Sorry, it was an accident." "I don't care if it was an accident; just watch where you're going, jerk!"

Consider another example about how it feels when driving a car and someone cuts you off the road. An earlier stage expression of anger is throwing up your hands in frustration or saying, "What an idiot!" Now, in this stage of anger, you blame the person for what happened and instead of being angry *about* it you aim your animosity directly at him. You yell out the window, "You idiot!" (You do not yet aim your car at him to ram his car—that comes from accusing the person of *intentionally* trying to hurt you.)

Anger that arises from blame becomes even more intense when the hostile person adds, "You people always do this to me and I've had it!" Generalizing "you people" elevates the danger of aggression, because it depersonalizes you and possibly reduces you to a denigrated group, making you appear less as an individual with real feelings or needs and thereby making it easier to hurt you (if the hostility is not defused and escalates in a violent direction). Depersonalization can even more forcefully come at you with accumulated antagonism from previously expressed feelings of belligerence toward "you people." Minority groups and other victims of discrimination (people of color, women, homosexuals, etc.) can tell you what it feels like when someone viciously says "you people!"

Another characteristic of hostility is that its intensity makes it more constant and unrelenting as opposed to short bursts of exasperation. There is no yelling and then lull, getting "in your face" and then backing away. You feel the meanness unabated, see it in an icy glare rather than an aggressive glance or in an obvious obscene gesture rather than a furtive one that flashes and disappears. The person might stop shouting for a moment, but the intensity continues, because it is a persistent part of who she is as a person and how she manages life's challenges (as opposed to being a momentary response to a frustrating situation). Unlike the boss I described earlier as being angry because of having a bad day, another boss's anger was constant: as if he was always having a bad day. He constantly criticized his workers and insulted their performances. He was the schoolyard bully who grew up to be an adult bully, who belligerently abused his power by demeaning others or compensated for his lack of genuine inner authority by being authoritarian. This did not fluctuate day to day: he was a mean man every day and a mean boss all the time. "He always has a chip on his shoulder!" "He gets angry so easily!" "He talks down to us all the time!"

A final distinguishing aspect of hostility is that a person can use it to manipulate. An acquaintance, Ryan, always found tangential excuses to become angry in order to orchestrate situations to his benefit. Once, he did not want to go to his boyfriend's family dinner one night and so rather than directly express his intentions, which he knew would lead to an argument, he became angry over something unrelated and, when his partner understandably questioned his inexplicable anger, Ryan became belligerent and stormed out of the house, successfully using his hostility to manipulate what he wanted. Another scenario with a hostile person may be: "You know you were supposed to take the dog out." "Sorry, I thought it was your turn." "My turn? Are you crazy? I can't take any more of your irresponsibility tonight so I'm going out—I will see you when I get back!"

Hostile Body Language

It is important to be able to recognize hostility in a person's physical appearance—clenched fists, a vicious stare or belligerent stance—because it can alert you to the intensity of the person's anger and thereby help prepare your intervention. "If looks could kill!" Recognizing antagonistic body language begins with remembering the earlier examination of the effect of anger on one's body. It starts with adrenaline-fueled blood surging to muscles, which gives the person at earlier stages of anger the energy to stand up for himself. But at these more aggressive later stages, this results in the tensing of one's body as if getting ready to fight. You can observe this tension in his facial muscles, in a furrowed brow or the biting of lips as well as in a clenched jaw, pressured speech or rigid shoulders. You might see his fists clenching and releasing as way of relieving the tightened muscles.

Look for a flush color in a belligerent person's face, which is the result of more blood flowing through the veins and the person's body becoming hotter. You should similarly be on alert for sweaty/wringing hands or perspiration on the face, which is in response to the person's body cooling itself by stimulating sweat glands. You might also look for the hostile person licking her lips due to dry mouth from accelerated breathing.

Equally important is to look at the angry person's eyes. They can often tell you what the person is feeling. Are they riveted on you, unwavering? Are the pupils enlarged, which might suggest drugs or an extreme state of agitation? Do they frighten you, either due to their menacing look or because they seem cold and emotionally detached from the aggressive manner in which they speak?

Recognizing intense physical expressions not only can alert you to the degree of aggression in the person, but can also remind you to look at how you respond to the aggression within your own body language. Your physical posture can reflect a defensive fight/flight response to a person's hostility that can make you appear aggressive. This is important, because just as you instinctually respond to a person's aggressive posture so too he responds to your body language, such as your arms crossed defensively on your chest or if you appear agitated and restless, the result of increased adrenaline in your blood due to his intimidation. He in turn becomes more hostile, with the result being a vicious cycle of increasing aggression. Remember the incident I described earlier when I was assaulted fifteen years ago by a client. For months thereafter I found myself becoming not only tense when someone became belligerent but also anxious when I noticed the other person could see the tension in me, which emboldened him (knowing his belligerence had an effect on me) to become even more hostile.

Be aware of your own physical response to the antagonistic person and as a result you will be able to address it in a way that minimizes any negative influence it might have on your attempt to de-escalate his anger. You find your fists clenched, notice your arms crossed on your chest or maybe think to yourself, *My heart is pounding* or *Why am I so anxious?* These physical reactions alert you to the need to slow yourself down, which you can do through any of the various means we discussed in chapter 1 that work for you: controlled breathing, counting to ten, positive self-talk, releasing muscle tension, etc. These have the effect of reversing your adrenaline-fueled aggression and calming your tense body so you do not appear threatening. You consciously relax your facial muscles and as a result you do not look rigid or you tell yourself to uncross your arms or loosen clenched fists and you do not appear so combative. All of this sends a message to the belligerent person that you are calm and in control.

Let's look at a few examples of your defensive physical response to the hostile person that, upon recognition, can be controlled and thereby contribute to calming the situation. First is eye contact. Just as a person's hostile staring can make you, at best, uncomfortable and more likely defensive or angry, staring back aggressively at the hostile person will make her more hostile. She will probably engage you in a staring contest and will not back down until either you concede or an altercation ensues. So when you feel yourself staring back at the hostile person tell yourself to stop, that it is not productive. Count to ten, step away, do what it takes to break the impasse before it escalates.

Do not stare at the hostile person, but do not be evasive in your eye contact either. The lack of looking someone eye-to-eye will make you appear afraid or intimidated. This will embolden his hostility, making him feel successful in scaring you. Instead, maintain comfortable eye contact, neither averting your eyes nor staring at the person. A culturally determined rule for comfortable eye contact is if the person maintains steady eye contact then you maintain steady *non-threatening* eye contact. This means a person at the frustrated stage should receive steady and reassuring eye contact while the hostile person should receive steady but firm and confident eye contact. Steady—but not fixated—eye contact will show the antagonistic person you are in control but are not controlling and thereby help to calm her anger. One of the reasons the earlier mentioned client struck Gayle the manager with whom he had a spiraling battle of venomous words was, as he told me later, "She kept staring at me as if to blame me."

Maintain good eye contact with the hostile person and do so while being at eye level, which means sitting if she is sitting. Standing while she is sitting makes the person feel as if you are towering over her and that she is being aggressively controlled.

In a similar manner, be aware of how you speak to the hostile person. A high-pitched tone may reflect nervousness as does a louder voice reflect imperiousness, while a cold tone suggests accusations. Whereas in earlier stages of anger you wanted to project a reassuring voice, now, with the hostile person, you want a firm voice—albeit not a punitive one—that clearly lets the person know his behavior is unacceptable.

Finally, and most importantly, is how you physically stand with the hostile person. Being "in your face" compels an instinctual fight/flight response in you to stand up to her. Your arms might be crossed on your chest, demonstrating your commitment to your space and your refusal to *give ground* to her intimidation. You will probably be *squared-off* directly in front of her in a confrontational stance. This comes across as, at minimum, a defensive response (though more likely as an aggressive one) and so will make her more hostile.

Standing your ground in response to a hostile person makes you too close to that person. *Too close* is a relative phrase. It varies from culture to culture. In Japan, for instance, standing close to each other is different from a European culture, where people stand farther apart. Regardless of one's background, all people have a physical comfort zone in relation to another's proximity. An angry person's comfort zone is reduced significantly. It was less an issue in earlier stages of anger when standing near the person was reassuring; closeness to the hostile person comes across as controlling. She needs more distance between you and her because she has less trust of you and feels a need to show who is in control. "Don't stand so close to me!"

How do you know if you are too close to the angry person? If your proximity makes the person more belligerent, step back enough so as to not to appear aggressive but not too far so as to appear weak. If she backs away, respect her need for distance. Otherwise she will feel threatened. A good rule is to stand at least an arm's length from an antagonistic person. This makes her feel more secure since you are out of immediate physical reach of her. Do not stand directly facing her. Standing squarely in front of her—even outside of her comfort zone—makes you seem somewhat more aggressive, as if in a "face-to-face" showdown, rather than if you are a little to the side (usually to the left of the person since most people are right-handed and will strike you from the right).

Of course, this "comfortable" distance between you and the

hostile person also means you have created a buffer zone in which you are at an arm's (or leg's) reach out of his striking distance. You are not yet in physical danger from the hostile person since his compulsion is intimidation and not, as in later stages, physical threats or violence. Even still, being safe is important so maintain an arm's/leg's distance from him.

If the antagonistic person walks quickly or aggressively toward you and seems to be coming too close, you need to politely but firmly tell her to stop. Refrain from saying, "Stop", which can come across as an aggressive command and cause her to react more hostilely. Instead, simply let her know she is as close as you want her to come. "Okay, that is close enough." Do not wait until she gets too close, making you feel she has invaded your space, and then tell her to back off, because by then you will feel threatened and your demand that she back away will feel confrontational to her.

On the other hand, you do not want too much distance between you and the hostile person. Standing too far away makes you appear timid and vulnerable, as if you are afraid of the person. This can embolden her hostility, making her feel her intimidation has successfully frightened or weakened you (as does your appearing anxious, tense, physically uncomfortable, etc.). So step back if she "gets in your face", but only an arm's length, which is something that lets her know you are still confidently and respectfully present but will neither be goaded into a confrontation nor retreat in fear.

Equally important to how you stand facing the person is where you stand if you are behind the person. It is quite simple: do not stand behind the person. Standing behind a hostile person or approaching from behind might feel to him as if he is having a trap sprung on him or is being attacked and so will escalate his belligerence.

Wherever you are standing, do not approach the hostile person quickly or suddenly, because it will feel challenging and cause an even more aggressive reaction. Also keep your gestures minimal so as not to appear as if you are about to make a physical move.

Sticking your hands in your pockets suddenly, for example, or turning around quickly can be interpreted as aggressive acts.

Another expression of physical proximity, and this one being *way* too close of a contact, is the temptation to touch the hostile person reassuringly. Resist the temptation. You might be able to touch a person reassuringly in earlier stages of anger, when a person's anger is a demand for validation, but touching a hostile person in an attempt to help calm him is a bad idea. Any touch will feel like an attack on him or an intrusion on his personal space.

I observed a man belligerently yelling at a restaurant server and almost physically gasped when I saw the server reassuringly put her hand on his shoulder and start to say they could resolve his problem peacefully. Before the server could even finish her sentence, the man aggressively pushed her hand away and viciously told her to never touch him. He could have just as easily hurt her. Do not touch the hostile person and instead maintain a comfort zone between you, compounded with confident eye contact and a firm voice.

If you find yourself with sweaty palms or clenched fists and, in spite of your best efforts are not able to calm yourself, nor are able to calm the hostile person, ask yourself two important questions: Do you feel the situation is "out of hand"? And if so, can you regain control? Can you ultimately defuse the hostile person or is she instead going to be violent? If either of these questions have you worried, then you should be prepared for even more intense and potentially pernicious anger.

Defuse Hostility

What do you do when a person is hostile or tries to intimidate you? First, stay calm. It is always important to stay calm in response to someone's anger, but at this stage it is exceptionally challenging. Remaining calm at earlier stages was relatively easy when you reminded yourself that the person's anger neither was to be taken personally nor feared. At this stage, however, it *is* personal and it *is* frightening. The hostile person blames you for what angers him or makes you feel bullied into doing something you do not want to do.

Fear sends your fight/flight instincts into aggressive overdrive, which earlier was suggested as impeding the effective de-escalation of an angry person who simply needs to be heard. At this stage, however, fear is a natural and even healthy response to animosity. We should have some fear when a person is belligerent toward us. Fear warns you to be vigilant to what might come, that the individual who is "in your face" probably will not hit you but is close enough and mean enough to hit you. You get the unsettling sensation that his intimidation is meant to make you feel that way.

Fear makes you more guarded, which is good, but you do not want fear to rule you, as it does when it makes you anxious and less confident in your ability to handle a hostile person. That is what he intends: for you to feel frightened so as to acquiesce to his intimidation. You need to be keenly aware of the hostility *and* at the same time stay calm so as to balance your adrenaline-driven response with a reasonable assessment of the situation.

A person who "gets in your face", for example, elicits a healthy self-protective response that can also make you more aggressive than you need to be, such as in inclining you to push the person away. That would be inappropriate and possibly pernicious. Intimidation is not suggestive of imminent violence. Physically pushing away this person is an aggressive, not defensive act. It is not about protecting yourself, especially when it escalates the situation; and it *will* escalate the hostile person. He "gets in your face" not only to get what he wants but also to test the boundaries, to see if you will panic or overreact. He might move toward you as if to strike you, but he only really wants to see if you flinch or can be intimidated. Overreacting gives him an excuse to turn what once was being "in your face" into hitting your face.

The earlier mentioned store clerk, Charlie, told me it took all his resolve to resist the urge to push away a customer who stood inches from him belligerently demanding a refund for a supposed defective product. He realized he was being tested to see how he would respond, as if the customer was daring him to push back and if not, then to acquiesce to his demand. He knew this consumer was not like those he described to me who were rude or who had been having a bad day. He actually felt intimidated by this man with a mean disposition. Charlie's instinct was to put his hands up to gesture that the customer back off, because he was physically too close, but Charlie knew, having learned from experience, that anything he did or said could be misconstrued and make the customer meaner. He instead remained calm and professional, reminding himself that the "customer was always right" even when this was untrue.

Hostility is about control. The person needs to bully or intimidate, because it *makes* you do what she wants and that is power. Power is what makes her feel in control. Unlike in the earlier defensive state when anger puffed her up so as to protect against feeling controlled by you, now, in this more intensive stage, there is no question in her mind that she is not going to be pushed around; the question is how hard she is going to push *you* around (though, again, emotionally, not yet physically). The intensity of the person's anger sends a clear message that she will not let you control her; she controls you. Her harsh words are not expressions of frustration to influence you and instead are meant to insult or pressure you and thereby make her feel she has control over how you feel and act. The mean customer described by Charlie was arrogant and belligerently demanding in order to make it aggressively clear that the "customer was always right" and that he was in control, not the store clerk.

Recall also the example of a driver whose car is cut off the road, as happened to Kim when a black SUV cut her off. This made her momentarily feel less in control of her driving and in response yelled at the person or "flipped him the finger." She did *not* do so out of earlier stage frustration but to scare him and in scaring him she regained the control he expropriated from her when he cut her off. The same is true of the earlier examinations of Tom's being denied his medication and Bart not receiving his Social Security benefit check. Tom no longer needed to hear that the receptionist was listening to his frustration and instead needed her to hear that he was "calling the shots." "You might think that I'm going to listen to your bullshit, but you are going to give me my medicine and I'm not leaving here until you do!" Similarly, Robin knew it was not frustration that was being expressed when Bart aggressively said, "You're going to find a way to get me my check and I don't care how long it takes!" She *was* intimidated and Bart, who moments earlier felt his control had been expropriated when denied his check, now was "back on top" by aggressively making her feel what he wanted her to feel. Rather than accept being controlled by others, these men and women's anger was meant to intimidate and thereby reclaim their control.

Recall again the scenario of Derrick, the husband whose spouse defensively reprimanded him for being late and then viciously yelled at him if he tried to get her to talk about why she was angry. The latter made her feel like he was intruding into her protected inner emotions and thereby was expropriating the control she needed to decide when and with whom she would be vulnerable. Aggressively "snapping" at him successfully made him stop trying to get her to talk about uncomfortable feelings and in the process not only reinforced the control she needed to exert over those feelings but also cemented her control over him.

If a person's hostility is what makes her feel in control then how do you defuse the hostility without diminishing that critical control and, as a result, exacerbating the anger that protects against the loss of control? Your attempt to abate the person's anger is experienced as stifling and even expropriating her control, thus causing her to become more antagonistic in order to hold on to it. Tom's anger originally compensated for the control he lost upon being told he could not get his medicine, but when he subsequently was told to stop the anger that made him feel in control, he then felt the control over his own life was jeopardized. So he became belligerent to maintain his control and to not let the receptionist control him. The dilemma of de-escalating hostility is that you do not want to expropriate the control that comes from anger, but you also do not want to be controlled by a person's verbal abuse or bullying. Defusing hostility therefore requires balancing the person's need to feel in control and your need not to be controlled. It means letting her know *you know* her anger is intimidating—which assures her of her control—*and* you will not be intimidated by it, which assures her of your control.

The first component of this equation lets the person know you understand she is *so* angry that she is not going to stop yelling or being in "your face" simply because you demand it. "I can see how angry you are!" This makes her think you "get" her anger. As a result she relinquishes some of the antagonism that comes from having to prove aggressively to you she is in control. Susie's anger at her husband Derrick's tardiness defended against his intrusion into her personal feelings. Her anger would have been less vicious if Derrick backed off confronting her anger and instead said he understood why she was angry and that he would make sure it did not happen again. The control over her inner feelings and who has access to them thus would not have been challenged and, as a result, could have resulted in her releasing a little of her hostility. A similar response to Tom about understanding his anger comes from not getting his medicine would have alleviated some of the anxiety he felt from Bonnie seemingly having expropriated his control by not giving him his medicine.

Letting the hostile person know you understand her anger, however, does not mean doing nothing about it or acquiescing to its demands. You do not want to be seen as weak or easily victimized, like the child whom the bully knows is vulnerable and so picks on. You do not want the person to think you will do anything to placate his hostility so as to keep him from getting angrier, again like the child who gives his lunch money to the bully. This simply emboldens the person's meanness. A common example is a battered spouse who does everything she can to appease her angry partner so he will not abuse her and he still hits her, because to him she seems so weak.

You instead need to stand up to the bully, to let the batterer know you will not be victimized, to stop the hostile person's intimidation. This means addressing *how* the person expresses her anger, unlike in earlier stages where you focused more on *what* angered the person. Now you have to directly confront the person's aggressive behavior, because it is mean or intimidating and needs to be constrained. But how do you do this without escalating the person's anger and possibly being hurt as a result? The child knows that if he refuses the bully he might be bullied further and the spouse knows that if she says no to the batterer she might be beaten. Confronting the antagonistic person with "I will not allow you to talk that way to me" or "Get out of my face" threatens the underlying control that comes from being belligerently "in your face" and so exacerbates the antagonism. "Yeah, well, I'm talking to you that way and if you want to see how I can really talk to you then just try to stop me!" "You think I'm too close now—wait until I show you how close I can get!"

How do you stop a person's hostility without challenging the control that comes from it and thereby making him meaner? In previous stages of anger we were able to rein in anger yet not expropriate a person's control by being supportive of her need to express anger. At this more aggressive stage, however, listening and being supportive do not, on their own, restrain a person's hostility. They can even be counterproductive. It is like encouraging an angry person to hit a punching bag: the earlier stage person hits the bag for a limited time and gets out his frustration, but the more the hostile person hits the bag the angrier he becomes and the more aggressively he hits the bag. You do not want to stifle this person's anger, but validating it stimulates yelling or bullying rather than keeping it temporary and contained. It turns it into a kind of a rehearsal for the big bang, a form of getting "pumped up" for the real show. The result is the person shouts louder and longer until the "bark" of anger that once made him stand up to make you better hear him eventually becomes the physical "bite" of violence.

Saying, for example, "You have every right to be angry, but it would help if you would lower your voice," was effective in earlier stages of anger, but now results in, "You don't like my voice? That's your problem!" And a supportive, "I can see why you are angry," as mentioned previously, will make the person feel in control but will *not* be met with, "At last someone understands why I'm angry" and so diminish the anger. Instead the person will respond with something such as, "You haven't heard the half of it!" When the earlier mentioned Derrick originally tried to be understanding of his wife's inexplicable anger toward him for being late—"I hear your anger"—she amped up the belligerence: "You hear my anger? I don't have to hear your stupid clichés. Get out of here!"

Laura, a psychologist, told me she had been nodding her head to demonstrate understanding to a client who said he was so angry he could smash the lamp next to him. Note he did not say "would" break the lamp and so this was not a threat. Saying he *could* break the lamp was close enough to a threat that it would not take much to push it into violence. He meant it to be that close so as to intimidate the psychologist. Laura's response of nodding her head might have been interpreted by a person at an earlier stage of anger as understanding his frustration, but it caused this person to break the lamp, because he saw it as her not knowing the intensity of his anger and instead condoning it. The failure to recognize and rein in anger that was meant to intimidate could ultimately result in Laura being broken and not just the lamp.

The solution to the dilemma of defusing hostility without endangering the angry person's sense of control while also not giving her license to be hostile resides in the tandem interaction of letting the person know you understand the ferocity of her anger *and* that you need her to rein it in. Think of a person who is aggressively "in your face." You want her to know you understand she "means business", but you also want her to know her close proximity is unacceptable. "I see you are really angry and you have the right to be, but getting in my face won't work with me." This statement does not challenge the person's right to be angry—as would be the case if you were to push her away or demand she back off—and so does not threaten her control. It lets her know you will not be intimidated and she needs to constrain how she expresses her anger. She thereby retains the feeling of being in control or "on top" of her situation and at the same time realizes she can be so without having to be aggressively "on top" of you. "I get your message loud and clear and I need you to stop yelling so we can work on it." You can apply this to a co-worker who tries to pressure you into doing what she wants. "I think you have a good idea, but give us a little space to discuss it rather than having to accept it immediately."

Let us go back to the case study of Bart, who is angry about not receiving his Social Security benefit. "I want my check and I'm not leaving until you get it for me!" Unlike the earlier stage person who leaves without the check once he is reassured, Robin, the social worker, is trying to help the hostile person who meanly dismisses her "lame excuses" for not getting his check and belligerently makes it clear he will not leave until he gets it. This aggressively makes him feel in control. Robin needs to quickly assert her own control otherwise Bart feels he can control her and so will not leave until she submits to his intimidation.

At the same time, anger is the hostile person's way of trying not to lose control. Your task, therefore, is to assert your control without making him feel you are trying to curtail his. In this way you neutralize the power struggle over who is in control. "Of course you have every right to expect good services and I'm going to do everything I can, so I need you to stop yelling and we'll mange this."

How would this apply to Tom and Bonnie or Derrick and Susie? Had Bonnie not criticized Tom and instead, as mentioned, let him know she realized his intense anger was about not getting his medicine, he would not have felt controlled *and* at the same time she could also have told him that he needed to restrain some of his belligerence. The same can be said of Derrick. Had he not confronted his wife's anger and instead expressed that he knew how angry his tardiness made her, she would have been less belligerent *and* at the same time he could have asked her to stop yelling so they could work on how to make sure he would be sensitive to being on time. Neither Bonnie nor Derrick would accept being abused with these responses and they would do so in a manner that neither threatened to expropriate control from the angry people nor diminish their own control.

Think of what you would do if you were sitting behind a desk in an office or waiting room and a person came around the desk and belligerently berated you. In most of these situations that I have observed, the worker demanded that the interloper move away from behind the desk, to which the person became more aggressive: "Make me!" Instead, you want to create a balance of the person's maintaining control and your asserting control: "I know you are angry and I want to help, but I need you to go back on the other side of the desk so that I can do my job." (A person who *charges* behind your desk in a threatening manner necessitates protecting yourself.)

One day on the way home from work I observed a person trying to get on a city bus who then became belligerent when the driver said he was sorry but that the passenger had to get off, because the bus was overcrowded. The driver's validation of the passenger's frustration would have defused the passenger's anger in earlier stages, but the hostile person aggressively refused to exit. The driver called him selfish for delaying everyone and said she could not go further until he got off the bus. The passenger still refused and meanly said, "Then no one's going anywhere!" I then asked everyone on the bus to step back a little so that we could fit him on the bus, which everyone did and we proceeded.

What should the bus driver have done differently? It was her job to be responsible for the passengers' safety and so she had to address the hostile person, but instead of calling him selfish, which might have been accurate but escalated his animosity, she could have recognized that the intensity of his anger suggested it was not just about getting on the bus but about something more. Maybe being told what to do made him feel controlled and triggered deeper resentment. Such awareness might have helped her respond differently to him. Instead of criticizing him, for instance, the bus driver could have said, "I know you want to get home"—which would have shown her understanding of his anger—and then could have added, "Everyone needs to get home, but because we are full and over the limit of allowed passengers, I need you to take the next bus, which is coming shortly."

Could the lesson learned from the bus driver and angry passenger be applied to the earlier described situation of the mean boss who criticized and imperiously commanded his workers? Workers cannot challenge the manner in which their boss supervises them, for any challenge to his authoritarian rule would almost certainly be met with, at best, a reprimand and, at worst, termination from their jobs. They could, however, acknowledge his legitimate authority in assigning their tasks—which would reaffirm his need to have his control respected—while at the same time suggesting they could perform their tasks more efficiently if they all cooperated rather than feeling weighed down by his orders. "I know you need this to be done correctly, but it would help if you gave me some suggestions rather than telling me what I am doing wrong." Charlie, the store clerk, told me he had handled his more intimidating customers in a similar way by saying, "You deserve the best service and if you would be so kind as to give me a little space I will be glad to provide that service for you."

Defuse Hostile Anger

Remember that a person's hostility is particularly resistant to being de-escalated when it arises at least in part from blaming you for what angered the person. Blame makes you if not an enemy then at least an adversary, one who causes the person's problems and so needs to be coerced to do what the person demands. You need to de-escalate the belligerence of the person's blame and do so not by an aggressive power struggle but by refocusing the person's attention away from you to the problem that angered her. That is, move her away from the "you" of "You did this to me" and toward talking about the problem. "You're understandably angry, because you didn't get what you asked for, but I need you to stop yelling and tell me what happened so we can figure out what to do." Maybe she responds, "Yeah, I didn't get it, so make sure you do it!" She still aggressively wants you to fix her problem, but at least she is talking about it instead of pointing a hostile finger at you for causing it.

You can also address the reason it was not you who caused the person's problem and instead, for example, that it was Social Security who denied him his check, but you will do what you can to help. In this manner, you show him you are not the enemy and thereby deflect some of his animosity away from you. A secondary benefit of getting the person to see you not as an adversary is that he will see you as an individual with real flesh and feelings, which diminishes his compulsion to depersonalize or demonize you and thereby more easily hurt you. You similarly encourage him to see you as a real person when you reinforce the "me": "Hey, you know me; I am trying to help so you don't have to yell." Or "I'm not one of those guys; I'm here to help, so stop cursing and let me help."

Do not, however, engage in an argument or become defensive about who is to blame. Refuting accusations or making excuses for your actions will escalate the person's animosity. It contradicts what the person says and makes him think you are calling him a liar. Or it results in an argument about who is right and he will win this argument through bullying. "You're trying to get out of it! You can give it to me and you know it!"

I watched a social worker, for example, try to explain to an antagonistic person that it was not her fault she could not give him what he wanted. He continued demanding it and the social worker continued explaining why she could not give it to him, but with each explanation the person got more antagonistic. "I don't want to hear you can't—just do it!"

Of course you do not want to accept blame and its accompanying wrath for something you did not do. You might try to explain why the person's animosity is actually based on a misunderstanding so he will not think it was your fault. Remember an angry person's heightened emotional state makes him less receptive to rational explanations. Do not expect a response such as, "Oh okay. I see why it's not your fault." Be prepared instead for an antagonistic reaction and try to respond to it in a way that is understanding rather than confrontational. "I know you feel it's my fault and that gives you reason to be angry..." Then ask the person to hear your perspective: "...if you would stop yelling for a moment and give me a chance to tell you what I'm thinking, you will see we can figure out what to do." Make it clear that not only have you not deliberately done anything to hurt him but also you have done everything you can to help. This is what the receptionist should have done with Tom. "I know you need your medications and I wish there was something more I could do to get them to you, but I have tried everything and unfortunately the doctor is gone for the day."

If, on the other hand, you take responsibility for the blame, let the person know you did not intentionally try to hurt him and that you are sorry. Be careful, however, how you apologize. You need to unequivocally apologize for mistakes at earlier stages because it validates the person's anger, but at this more intense stage of hostility you must be cautious in how you apologize, because it can make you appear weak. It can make the hostile person feel you are beholden to him for your mistake and thereby give him more reason to expect acquiescence. You instead want him to know your apology is sincere, which makes him feel in control, but it does not mean you are any less in control. So be confident when you apologize and move it from "sorry" to a constructive "Sorry that happened. Let's get it corrected now." Or in the situation of Derrick whose wife was angry at his tardiness: "Sorry. I know it's wrong to be late and if you give me the chance I will tell you how I am going to correct it."

There are a few things you must keep in mind when attempting to defuse a hostile person's anger.

First, do not threaten the hostile person with consequences. Do not tell your mean co-worker he needs to stop being belligerent or else you will take it to his supervisor. Do not tell the bully who is pressuring you to do something you do not want to do that you are going to call the police. You will need to intervene with consequences in the next stages of anger, but at this point it will be interpreted by the hostile person not only as proof you do not understand his anger but also as a challenge to his need to be in control: "Go crying to the boss—see whom she will believe!" "Go ahead call the police!" Now you either have to back down, which will embolden him, or act on your threat. If the latter, your complaint to your boss will be negated by your co-worker's turning it around to make you appear to be a complainer or your report to the police will be of little consequence since the person did not threaten you. These responses will escalate the person's antagonism and possibly push him to become meaner or even violent before the police arrive.

Instead of threatening consequences, help the person see the repercussions of her behavior. "There seems to be a lot of hostility here that is not going to get our work done so let's get past it." Or "Yelling is disturbing people and someone will call the police and we don't want that so let's calm down and work on the problem." This sets limits without threatening the person and therefore without making her angrier. But if she says, "I don't care if it doesn't get done, because you're doing it wrong anyway" or "I hope someone does call the police," then respond, "You might not care, but I don't want it so come on, please stop yelling and we can work on the problem." Keep trying to do whatever it takes to prevent further escalation of the hostility.

Further, be clear when you warn a person about the consequences of unacceptable behavior. You do not want ambiguity or confusion around it. "What do you mean you told me you I'd be denied services if I yelled at you? You never said that!" Present your limits simply and concisely, keeping in mind that the angry person might have a low comprehension and attention span. Do not set limits that are unreasonable or punitive: "If you yell like a spoiled child you will be treated like a child!"

Be sure the limitations you set are manageable. Do not create restrictions you will not be able to enforce if the person continues to act out or which make him feel you would never go that far and so continues to act out. This is important, because the hostile person might test those limits to determine your breaking point. Be firm when you set these limits, because the person will transgress them if she feels she can and will not respect you or any limits you set. That is why if you say you will call security, be prepared to do it. Gayle, the manager in the increasingly hostile shouting match with a client, said she would call the police if the client continued disrespecting her to which the client responded by saying, "You're going to call the police because you have a fat ugly nose?" He knew it was unlikely that she would call the police or that the police would do anything even if they were summoned.

Second, you can do your best to defuse the hostile person, but some people simply will be belligerent or intimidating no matter what you do. This could include people who hate you simply because you are a person of color, a homosexual, a foreigner or any type of "other" that becomes the target of their animosity. These individuals' anger defines who they are and you will not be able to change them. Instead, try to deflect a prejudiced person's meanness away from being directed at you. "You certainly are entitled to your opinion and I believe I am also, so let's just get past this since we are not going to agree." Then be prepared to protect yourself if the bigotry intensifies and do not give any excuse for the person to escalate her hostility.

Third, be aware of others who are present when you are trying to de-escalate the hostile person. Other people can influence the way a person behaves. They might have a positive effect on the belligerent individual in that they can make him mindful of behaving properly in front of them. But more likely they will have the opposite effect, bringing out in him a wish to impress them or even to receive some sadistic pleasure in humiliating you in front of an audience. The earlier discussed authoritarian boss normally did not have one-on-one supervisorial meetings and instead seemed particularly to enjoy berating his workers in front of their co-workers.

Others' presence can also make a person feel he cannot back down from his belligerence. Other people might inhibit him from compromising or capitulating, as if this makes him appear weak. They particularly make him conscious of not wanting to appear to be controlled or to "lose face." Bystanders also could actually encourage the person to act on his animosity. Therefore, move a hostile person away from others' influence to a neutral environment. Being away from others rids that part of a person's aggression that is motivated by showcasing in front of others and thereby allows him to be less resistant to your intervention.

Remember, however, the same can be said for you when others are present as you try to defuse an antagonistic person. You do not want to be embarrassed or appear out of control in front of them and you might overreact to the angry person as a result. So it is good to remove the antagonistic individual from the crowd both for her sake and for yours. (Being alone with the hostile person is acceptable at this stage.)

Beware of removing a person from others when her animosity is aimed at them: it can now be redirected at you. For example, separating two people who are belligerently arguing or fighting allows you to talk with one away from the other and helps you calm the one due to diminishment of the aggression perpetuated when the two were in direct conflict. The problem is that the person you are trying to calm might displace the adrenaline-driven animosity invested in that interaction onto you. This is a fairly common experience for police or social workers who separate participants in domestic disturbances. Suddenly two people who were in an altercation forget about their mutual discord and turn belligerently toward the one doing the separation in order to defy that person's interrupting their altercation. Sometimes they even come to the defense of the other person who moments earlier they were battling. Be prepared for this possibility.

SIGNS OF HOSTILITY

Hostile people express their anger two ways: verbally and physically. Making a mental checklist of both outlets of anger will help you quickly indentify when a person has reached this stage of anger and is trying to push you into giving him what he wants.

Verbal	Physical
• Mean	• Clenched fists
• Intimidating	• Vicious stare
• Attacking	• Belligerent stance
• Standing up against you	• Furrowed brow
• Emotionally hurtful	• Biting and/or licking lips
• Blames you	• Clenched jaw
• Generalizing	• Rigid shoulders
• Unrelenting	• Flush in color
• Manipulative	• Sweaty/wringing hands

Be sure you do not in turn mimic any of this behavior; it will only make the hostile person angrier.

- Reflect on a time when you exhibited some of these behaviors. What calmed you down?
- What are some ways you can prevent a hostile person's attempts at bullying or intimidating you from succeeding?

CHAPTER 6

Rage

A firm approach helps restrain a person's aggressive behavior, but it causes some people to become even more aggressive in order not to be controlled. It prompts others to explode in rage when they lose control over the anger they previously managed by aggressively trying to control you. Anger is not the problem with rage; it is anger that is uncontrollable that is the problem. Rage is not merely an extreme expression of a person's anger, but an anger one cannot manage. Ranting is not simply venting and instead is bursting forth feelings the person cannot contain or are slipping out of her grasp. "I'm losing it!" "I'm going to blow my top!"

Psychiatry refers to some people who are prone to rage as having explosive personalities or intermittent explosive disorder. These people have impaired impulse control or difficulty discerning the difference between *feeling* angry and having to scream out that anger. Maybe they learned in childhood to repress anger, because it was "bad" and as a result never developed the psychological skills to express it in controlled and constructive manners. This is not a problem as long as they do not have to feel angry. But inevitably something angers them and their inability to manage it makes them feel emotionally flooded with its unabated intensity, culminating in feeling overwhelmed by a strong impulse to erupt in a "fit of rage."

I was surprised by my acquaintance Emily, who was always happy until one day, while trying to park her car, another driver pulled into a place before her and she screamed at him as if he had performed a horrific act. I told her we would find another parking place and she continued her tirade, ranting uncontrollably. When I asked her why the other driver had made her so angry, she turned her fury on me and demanded that I get out of the car.

A few weeks later I saw Emily again, who apologized to me for her outburst. She attributed it to a bad temper, one that historically had always had disastrous effects on her relationships. After she told me more about herself and what instigated these outbursts, I recognized the symptoms of an inability to control impulses coupled with a "short fuse."

I realized she was almost always happy as long as everything went her way, which she always made sure would happen. This had created a type of insular emotional bubble, one in which her gratification was always paramount and assured, with the result being that everything was perfect until reality intruded with some problem—small or large—and burst her bubble. It had to burst her bubble, because her need for immediate gratification orientation to life meant she always expected and experienced an advantageous outcome to situations and so she never learned how to directly manage unfulfilled gratification. She never developed the confidence in herself to say, "That was disappointing" or "I'm frustrated," as well as the subsequent internal strengths to manage the frustration. If she had developed those emotional strengths, she would have maintained control of her feelings and would have assertively told the driver who took her parking space that he was selfish or something to that effect.

She did not know how to express feelings of deprivation and especially did not know how to manage them and so when they happened, when someone like the driver intruded into her perfect world, it was a sharp pin prick that burst its bubble. Life was all or nothing, perfect calm that comes from gratification or rage that comes when that gratification is denied and the resulting feelings of loss cannot be managed. Either the bubble is perfectly gratifying or the bubble is burst and she erupts in uncontrollable rage. She cannot simply reprimand the inconsiderate driver for unknowingly bursting her bubble and instead projects a fusillade of obscenities at him for what he did.

Enraged people are not all like this acquaintance. They are not necessarily inherent of an "explosive disorder" and instead are more typically the ones described as volatile, hotheaded, bad-tempered or short-fused. Unlike in earlier stages when a person's yelling safely vents feelings or defends against being vulnerable, the anger brews and builds beneath a veneer of restraint or within the hostility that maintains his control until, often without warning, he feels overwhelmed by the unmanageable anger and explodes in rage (or what might be described as a regressive temper tantrum). That potential lack of warning can make you unprepared for the fury and thus vulnerable to danger.

Remember Susie who became hostile about her husband Derrick's tardiness, because it made her feel unappreciated. Her hostility was meant to push him away when he insisted on talking about her feelings. When instead he said he had "had it" with her meanness and it had to stop, she "snapped" and exploded in rage. Her hostility had failed to push him away and as a result made her feel stripped of control: both over him and over the unmanageable vulnerability he made her feel. So she became apoplectic, screaming, "I can't take it anymore!" The ironic result is that his intrusive confrontation of her feelings stopped, though not because of resolving their untenable crisis and instead because her rage had such intensity to it that it made him back away from her feelings in fear.

The same trajectory from frustration to hostility to fits of fury can be witnessed in some of our other frequently discussed situations. Remember Carl, the man who felt vulnerable during a false fire alarm and so became angry at the manager when she told him to stop yelling and control himself. He did the opposite, panicking at the overwhelming feelings of vulnerability and began ranting uncontrollably. "Why are you doing this to me?" Also consider that Tom's failure to intimidate the receptionist into giving him his medicine made him anxiously know he would not be able to get through the night without receiving his prescription. Knowing he had absolutely no control over the situation, he became overwhelmed by how it made him feel and began to rant uncontrollably about what was going to happen to him.

"Blowing up" or "going ballistic" is not manipulative, though a person may feel a desperate attempt of craziness will make you capitulate to his demands. It is simply a feeling of being overwhelmed and out of control. It does, however, benefit the person in that rage sometimes results in attaining one's goal (Derrick did stop confronting Susie's anger, for instance). It can also induce a cathartic sense of relief as when an outburst of obscenities or irrational ranting indulges an internal compulsion to be free of constraints and to relieve the pressure-cooker of intense and at times overwhelming feelings.

The intense release of anger can be akin to the "rush" of drugs. The enraged person normally works desperately at maintaining control of her feelings, even being belligerent or mean to maintain her rigid order, and then experiences a "high" that comes with relinquishing control and "going crazy" or "letting it all out." The ecstatic pouring forth of pent-up feelings even is addictive: the colloquial expression of a rageaholic.

The rageaholic not only gets "high" from the intense release of buried feelings, but also is driven by—and becomes addicted to—the adrenaline that anger activates. Adrenaline contributes to the surge of excitement the enraged person feels. It further is a factor in the physical release the rageful person experiences when the tense feelings in the adrenaline-fueled muscles suddenly let loose in an explosive outburst. Subsequently comes the relief a person experiences when anger subsides, when adrenaline recedes and she feels a comfortable calm that comes from the abatement of excitement. All of this can be so addictive that it becomes a compelling motivation to become enraged. The person seeks situations that can make her angry or finds seemingly insignificant incidents to trigger the sublimely self-satisfying rage.

Cheryl, a woman I know, had a rigidly ordered world of work and family that resulted in her feeling bored, even depressed. This boredom was transcended when periodically she went apoplectic over some small or large problem and felt relaxed after her fury subsided. The "high" instigated by her rage and the pervasive relief after it climaxed caused her to unknowingly—or so it seemed—seek and even create situations that incited her to become enraged. Therefore, minor misunderstandings were blown up into catastrophes so as to allow her to blow up. The small incident that allowed her to become furious, in a self-fulfilling prophecy, became catastrophic due to the effect on it of her rage.

Like any addicted person, a rageaholic can build a tolerance to what enrages him. That which currently makes him furious eventually becomes insufficient to feed the "rush" he gets from being enraged. He is compelled to "score" a new fix to impede the inevitable "crash" of coming down from his vehement "high", which he does by escalating the anger that maintains his "high" or by finding a new problem that triggers another outburst. Cheryl increasingly turned small and smaller incidences into reasons to become enraged or twisted people's reactions to the inappropriateness of her anger into furious accusations that they were attacking her for her feelings.

The enraged person does not want to relinquish the anger that keeps her "high" and therefore is not receptive to de-escalation. You might think you have done everything to rein in her rage yet it remains unabated, because she is motivated more by the angry "fix" of rage than she is by wanting to resolve the situation that triggers it. And not only is she unreceptive to de-escalation, but also she is dangerous: not just from rage's sudden eruption that catches you unprepared but because the compulsion to score a new "fix" can drive her to do whatever it takes to gratify her cravings, to the point of violence if necessary. It is your task, as difficult as it is, to help control her rage before it reaches that point.

Control Rage

Enraged screams of "I'm going to lose it" or interminable ranting warn you the person is out of control. He slams the door *not* to get your attention—as in earlier stages—but because he is not in control of his feelings. Screaming or slamming the door can be a desperate plea for you to provide the control the person cannot exhibit himself. He probably knows his ranting is going on too long or his screaming is out of control, but he cannot stop it and anxiously feels it is slipping out of his grasp. He needs you to save him from himself. Think of the classic image of an enraged person who stands up to fight another man—"Let me at him!"—but who, deep inside himself, is grateful when friends hold him back, because he lacks the control to do so himself. Your control is like those friends holding back the person's fury.

Restoring control is the salient issue in de-escalating rage. The person might find some addictive relief in the "high" of being enraged, but she is also afraid of how being out of control makes her feel unsafe, chaotic, "out of her mind" and even a danger to you as well as to herself.

Your challenge is to help the person retract her rage and restore the order she cannot assert herself. This task begins with your staying in control. A person's explosiveness or ranting can be unnerving and even frightening. You need to remain calm and not overreact to rage. Staying calm demonstrates to the person who is out of control that you are in control.

If the enraged person views you as afraid to handle her rage or as not even trying to rein in her rage, she thinks you are not in control of the situation. She takes your reticence or fear as if you either condone or cannot control her irrepressible behavior. If she feels you condone it, she thinks you have given in to her temper tantrum, which perpetuates ranting as an effective tool in achieving what she wants. If you do not constrain her rage, she thinks you are incapable of dealing with it, thereby reinforcing the anxiety that her anger is unmanageable.

Defuse Rage

Danielle, a therapist I know, has a husband, Isaac, who periodically erupts in rage. Danielle demands greater maturity from Isaac than handling conflict so "childishly," as she puts it. Telling him he is childish fuels his rage, which she knows, and she regrets saying this to him every time she says it. She did not originally call his outbursts childish and instead took the time to explain to him that they were emotional responses to "bumps" in his daily path that he could learn to manage better. When time proved that he could not—or would not—learn to deal with these bumps in a more mature manner and instead continued to become enraged whenever he hit a bump, she became exasperated. That is when she began telling him his rage was a "childish tantrum"—often in a tone that was not very different from his fury—and that he needed to grow out of it. Isaac is not receptive to her critical assessment and Danielle in turn says she has "had it" with his outbursts: all of which further enrages him.

My advice to Danielle was to stay calm and is what I have continuously suggested to you, which will help you remain in control of your feelings when confronted with a person's rage. That is the first step to helping the person gain control over his enraged feelings. Staying in control will send a critical message to the furious person that not only are *you* not overwhelmed by his angry chaos but also you will not let *him* be overwhelmed either. "I know it feels crazy right now, but I promise we are going to get on top of it." This helps "put the lid" on the explosive feelings that he cannot do himself. When he screams "I'm losing it" or "I can't take it anymore", get him to focus on you and your effort to bring his feelings under control. "Isaac, look at me; I assure you I have dealt with these kinds of situations and we are going to get through this." Firmly saying the person's name is not inconsequential. It is a small step to bringing him back from being out "out of his mind" with rage to being more concrete oriented.

My acquaintance Emily, whom I mentioned earlier, became enraged when the driver of another car pulled into a parking space before her. Telling Emily to take it easy and that there would be another parking space was of no help and made her even angrier. It was not the parking space availability or the lack thereof that caused her rage. It instead was the other driver's expropriating her control and bursting the bubble of her immediate need for gratification orientation to life. She did not need someone to tell her that there would be another parking spot or that her anger was inappropriate; what she needed to hear was that in spite of not getting the parking spot she wanted, her rage was not going to become out of control and that she was going to be okay. "I'm glad he didn't do that to me, but I know you and you can handle this without getting out of control."

Demonstrating control and helping the enraged person know that her feelings are more manageable than she believed them to be can make her feel a little safer with overwhelming feelings, but it does not do so effectively unless you simultaneously set strict limits to her rage. Your approach is not just "It's going to be okay" but rather "It's going to be okay and so the rage has to stop." The person can begin to curb the ranting, because the safety she feels from your external control helps her know the situation really is okay and her intense feelings can and need to be controlled. "Emily, look at me; this is manageable, so I need you to get a hold of yourself and we are going to get on top of this." Emily will feel she can cope with her feelings rather than be overwhelmed by them and so will lessen some of her fury.

Firmly let the enraged person know that her ranting has gone on too long or that her fit of rage will not be tolerated. However, *firm* does not mean demanding the person stop ranting. Telling a person to stop her uncontrollable rage is like telling a child to cease a temper tantrum. It does not subside the ranting and instead makes her yell more. It makes her feel criticized or faulted when she probably already feels a certain amount of shame for ranting and for lacking the maturity to control her emotions and so she feels both further embarrassed and further compelled to rage.

That is why Tom, who was angry at the receptionist for not giving him his medication, "went nuts"—as he described it afterwards—when Bonnie tried to explain it was not her responsibility he was late and he had to stop screaming. "So it's my fault I am going to go crazy, because you will not give me my medicine. I can't take it anymore!" Bonnie instead could have firmly let Tom know he needed to rein in his rage while also letting him know he could manage it. Also remember the case of Susie who "snapped" when her husband Derrick told her to stop ranting and who would have responded more positively had he instead told her he understood her anger and that they could work through what angered her if she would stop yelling and let him tell her how he was going to do it. Both Susie and Tom would then have felt safer downsizing some of their storming rage.

Once I observed an angry customer at an airline counter ranting about the horrible worker who "lost" her assigned window seat. The agent apologized and the more he explained that the window seats were all occupied and so he could not give her the one she requested, the shriller the customer became. The agent tried to tell the angry woman that the reservationist probably made a mistake or hit a wrong button, but his logical explanation spun the customer into a "blind rage." What the agent probably did not know is that anger at all stages makes a person think less logically—even more so the enraged person—and thereby put this woman into a hyper-emotional state where his explanations of what happened would neither be cognitively processed nor reasonably responded to. The enraged person hears what is said through the filter of being so angry that she cannot "think straight" or is "out of her mind." Any such explanations of why the customer was not going to get her assigned seat were not only incomprehensible but also infuriating to her. The agent responded to the customer's increasingly manic ranting by demanding she stop, which made her rant more furiously. Hearing the agent say, "I need you to stop yelling" resulted in the customer screaming, "And I need you to give me my assigned seat!"

The agent should have recognized from the raw intensity of the woman's rage that his first task was not to tell the customer to stop ranting and instead to help her regain some control over her anger. Without a modicum of control the customer would be impossible to assist and would ultimately lose control altogether, as she demonstrated when the agent said he would have to call security if she did not stop screaming and she said, "Oh yeah, well tell them to bring a straight jacket because that is the only way you are getting me out of here!" The agent did not know the underlying psychological issues that made this woman explode emotionally, that she had impulse control problems and was living in an idealized bubble that burst whenever she was disappointed. But he could have learned from experience that when a person's anger is so intense and seemingly out of control, she needs help regaining control rather than being told to stop screaming. The agent needed to make the enraged woman feel the situation was manageable, that he was not going to let her overwhelming anger either make her lose control or get in the way of him helping get her on the plane. He could do this not by arguing with her or demanding acquiescence but rather by saying it was lousy she lost her assigned seat and he certainly would look into how it happened, but at that moment he knew her priority was to get on the plane, because it was departing and so he needed her to stop yelling and let him do his job. She would have allowed him to do his job, because he made her feel the situation *was* manageable and thereby made her feel less overwhelmed.

A simple reassurance that you want to help and not hinder the enraged person goes a long way in making her more receptive to the limits you subsequently set on her rage: "Let me assure you I am here to help and so I am asking you to control your anger and let me help." Or directly let the person know when her ranting has gone on long enough and is hindering your helping her: "I can see how angry you are, but at this point it is not resolving anything so it is time to stop yelling and let's concentrate on how to fix the problem." This statement does not exacerbate the person's rage, because it does not feel like criticism, as would saying "You're going on too long" or "You're all over the place!" Instead, saying, "I know you're angry, but you seem to be talking about several things at once so would you respond *only* to this one thought" helps the person constructively focus attention and thereby feel more in control and less enraged.

Two important caveats need to be stated to conclude the discussion on rage. First, the enraged person is less rational and less in control and as a result can be unpredictable. He can "fly off the handle" at any moment and actually hurt you. So be vigilant. Second, do not expect all intensely angry people to be irrational and emotionally explosive: some are very logical and methodically plan how to use their anger to threaten you to get what they want.

STAY IN CONTROL

People expressing rage are not in control of their feelings. When defusing an angry person in this stage, you must help them regain control. One important aspect of accomplishing this is to remain in control of yourself. Avoid negative thinking, which may cause you to panic and feel you are losing control. Here are some reflective exercises to change negative thinking into positive self-statements:

- Consider a time when you stopped a negative thought. How did you refute it?
- Role-play by yourself or with a friend a situation of a person expressing rage. Be sure to use positive self-statements throughout.
- Reflect on a circumstance that you found difficult, made you anxious or had a disagreeable outcome.
- Change your current negative thoughts about this event into positive self-statements.
- Use the new positive statements whenever the occasion comes up in your memory or in conversation.

CHAPTER 7

Threats

Some people become enraged when their anger does not control you, while others double their aggressive efforts in order to control you. My acquaintance Emily "went crazy" when the driver took her parking space, but she did not aggressively confront him as did another driver, Chris, who was cut off by a motorist and drove furiously to catch up to him and then yelled at him to pull over or he would ram his car. A person's irrepressible rage might have been unnerving, albeit not to the extent to make you lose control of the situation; but whereas a person's intimidation had enough ambiguity in it that you did not feel sufficiently scared to submit to its hostility, any hint of subtlety is abandoned when you are unambiguously threatened. What once was a hostile "Give it to me" is now "Give it to me or I will hit you!" A slamming of a book on a desk that previously was meant to intimidate now clearly delivers the message that you are next to be hit. A bullying, "I will not take no for an answer" is replaced with consequences: "You *will* do it or else!" A person who is "in your face" in order to see if you will flinch is now going to hit your face if you do not comply with his demands. And where previously a person's anger defensively implied "don't go there" if you got too emotionally close, there is now an aggressive "don't go there if you know what is good for you!"

Let us revisit Bart, the man who tried to intimidate the social worker with "I will not leave this office until I get my check!" In contrast to him, who in the end would leave the office even if the worker was not intimidated, the angry person at this next stage of anger means it when he warns, "I'm not leaving here without my check and if that means someone is going to get hurt then that is what it takes!" If the worker says she wishes she could help but she cannot, he will respond with, "You will find a way or I will make you find a way!" The same development transpired with the previously discussed client Tom who, when intimidation failed to convince the receptionist to get him his medicine, said, "I don't care what it takes, but you are going to get me my medication or you will regret that you didn't!"

Anger's sixth stage is a crisis. Whereas in earlier stages, anger was the expression of a person who *stands up to you* so as not to be pushed around and later to hostilely push you around, now the person's anger makes him stand up *to tower over* you in order to threaten *physically* to push you around. He is driven from a belief that he has done all he can and so, pushed to his limits, he has no other way to make you comply with his expectations except that of threatening harm. "I'll hurt you if you don't give it to me!"

Threats can be somewhat veiled: "Something bad is going to happen if I do not get my…" They can be obvious: "I will smack you if you don't do what I say!" Either way, threats are dangerous: you know you will be harmed if you do not produce the desired results.

Threat Assessment

How do you know whether to take the person's threat seriously? The answer is to take all threats seriously. Something inside the human psyche normally inhibits people from hurting others, but sometimes anger and aggression combine in a lethal explosion and a last step before transgressing normal constraints against violence is a warning that it is going to happen.

You might be tempted for any number of reasons not to take the threat seriously. You might, for example, be accustomed to a particular person's repeated acts of "crying wolf" and so not believe it. Or you might think someone's threat is merely a bluff to get what he wants, that he really does not have the fortitude to back up what he says and so you call him on it. The "wolf" might be real, however and calling the person's bluff might result in his not backing down and instead hurting you.

How do you know the difference between an idle threat that is meant to make you acquiesce without any intention to actually hurt you and a real threat that will inflict harm if not adequately heeded? There are several signs which taken individually or collectively can indicate a person's likelihood of acting on a threat. Violence is usually not random and instead can be preceded by eight warning signs. Recognizing them should infuse your approach to the threatening person with a great amount of concern for your safety (and with an equally critical amount of insight into how to defuse that threat).

Warning Signs a Threat is Real
1. Blames You
2. Perceives Threats as the Only Choice
3. Threatens Obsessively
4. Expresses Agitated Body Language
5. Presents a Plan to Harm
6. Has a Predisposition to Violence
7. Disregards Warnings
8. Is Under the Influence of Alcohol or Drugs

1. Blames You
The possibly most significant indication a person is likely to act on her threat is she blames you for what angers her. The earlier section on hostility examined the manner in which blame made a person's anger more intense, because it transforms an expression of frustration into a verbal attack against you for causing that frustration. Now, the person accuses you of causing her frustration not only by

withholding what she needs but also by *intentionally* withholding it. You did it on purpose. You could have helped her "If you really wanted to!" By not helping the person, she feels you chose to deliberately, even maliciously, hurt her. So she feels justified in threatening to hurt you in order to get that for which you hurt her. She does not necessarily want to harm you—as in an act of retaliation for hurting her, which we will see in the final stage of anger—but she lets you know you need to stop hurting her by giving her what she needs or she will hurt you.

Chris, the driver mentioned earlier who threatened the motorist who cut him off the road, was angry *not* because he was frustrated or that the motorist was a bad driver but because he blamed the motorist for almost getting him killed. That anger compelled him to drive quickly to catch up to the driver and warn him to pull over or he would ram his car. The threat took on even greater intensity when there was added to it a sense of almost daring the person not to acquiesce, as if that is what Chris wanted so as to have a reason to act on his threat. Carrying out a threat would bring him to the final stage of violence, in which Chris really did ram the motorist's car when he did not pull over or "kicked his ass" as threatened when he did pull over. The threat was real!

Consider another earlier example of being in a crowded situation and you accidentally bump into a person who becomes angry, only now before you even have a chance to apologize he threatens you: "Watch where you're going or I'll watch for you!" You could apologize in earlier stages of anger and the person's defensiveness or hostility would diminish. The threatening person, however, is not mollified by your apology. This is because he sees the bump not as an accident—even with your apology and exclamation that it was an accident—and instead as something either overtly intentional or at least due to being inconsiderate. "Do it again and I'll show you what it is like to bump someone!"

2. Perceives Threats as the Only Choice
A person's threat is real when she perceives threatening you to be her *only choice*. Yelling and intimidation did not make you acquiesce

and so she thinks she has no alternative but to threaten you to get what she needs. It expresses a sense of desperation: of having waited too long for you to resolve her problem, of having tired of coping with the situation, of having reached the end of her patience and of having no resolution in sight or other way out. You can hear in her voice she is resigned to not getting what she wants, or similarly, is resigned to doing whatever it takes to get what she wants. "I'm done talking; either do it or I'm going to hurt you!" Or more succinctly, "You leave me no choice!" More dangerous is when the resignation includes a fatalistic sense that since she is not going to win then she is going to make you lose with her. "If I have to suffer then you're going to suffer too!" Susie's anger at her husband Derrick's tardiness was clearly her way of pushing him away, only to have him insistently push back with his desire for her to process her anger toward him. She finally felt "at the end of my rope" and threatened that unless he "back off" she would back him off.

Threatening you because there is no alternative becomes more pernicious when the person feels he cannot back down from that threat. If his warning is intended to impress others, if peer pressure weighs heavily on him to follow through with his threat or if self-respect is at stake because of it, he will probably not risk "losing face" by not acting on his threat. He has started something he has to finish. Remember the client's escalating shouting match with the manager, Gayle, who had to have the last word. In the end the client threatened that if Gayle did not stop telling him what to do then he would hit her. He made the threat in front of others and so, when Gayle neither had the skills to recognize the seriousness of his threat nor the common sense to stop the shouting match, the client, pressured by his peers to not back down from his threat, hit her.

3. Threatens Obsessively

A warning that a threat is serious is not only the desperation you hear in the person's threatening words but also how he speaks them. He seems obsessed about his threat rather than simply stating it. He cannot let go of how hurt he feels and keeps saying he has been wronged or that he should not have been fired. "You'll pay for this!" He might also make repeated references to how he has hurt others or will hurt you. "I didn't take it from her and I won't take it from you!" It might even feel like bragging. "He didn't think I had it in me, but I showed him what I'm made of!" The longer the person's threat continues and the louder it becomes, the more clearly it is building toward a violent climax.

You get a sense that a threat is inevitably leading to violence from someone who talks to you as if threatening you is normal. This person does not view threatening behavior as something extraordinary, like someone who says "I really don't like doing this, but you leave me no choice." He instead seems to suggest that violence is his typical way of resolving issues. He is willing to do what it takes to get what he wants and if that means hurting you then that is the natural next step.

4. Expresses Agitated Body Language

Mounting tension is also manifested in the threatening person's increasingly agitated body language. His breathing becomes heavier or faster, for example, as if he is pumping himself up for action. Or he lowers his head a little, as when a person drops his chin in a fight (lowering the chin is an instinctual way to protect the neck as well as to make oneself less of a physical target by being more compact). The person might also become more physically "in your face" or move closer within your comfort zone, which is *too close* and is too accessible to hitting you if he acts on his threat, and he will not back off when you ask him to do so.

Maybe you see something change in the person's eyes, a look that suggests he is becoming more desperate and determined. Maybe instead he has a blank stare, giving you a sense that you have lost him and he is capable of doing anything. Or maybe he is looking you up and down, sizing you up as if trying to assess how to attack you. He might be looking about frantically—or furtively—for something, maybe for some kind of a weapon to use if he has to hurt you.

Rather than looking for a weapon, the person might have one with him. Maybe he is not exhibiting his weapon and instead claims he has one you do not see or boasts of having access to a weapon or having used one in the past.

While a person might increase her threat's intensity by pulling out a weapon or yelling more aggressively, she might escalate the threat in the opposite direction. She suddenly stops yelling or being physically threatening. You might think she finally has become calm or reasonable when instead she is contemplating a preemptive strike to hurt you before you have time to realize she is serious about her threat. This makes the threatening person particularly dangerous, because her sudden calm can fool you into lowering your guard.

5. Presents a Plan to Harm

Another very clear sign that indicates a person's threat is likely to be acted on is when she presents an actual plan of hurting you. She has moved the threat from generalizations—"Someone's going to pay for this" or "You people aren't going to get away with this anymore"—to a very concrete statement: "I'm going to hurt you if you don't..." Threats that are not only concrete but also specific are even more dangerous. "I will get you for what you did" is fairly concrete, but adding "I have my gun in the car and I will get it if you don't... " is even more specific. Similarly, saying, "I will blow up everybody" is a serious threat, but you have more reason for concern if it is specific as well as realistic: "I know how to make a bomb from my days in the army and I will be back with one if you don't..." Giving you a countdown is also concrete and specific: "I'll give you until ten and then I'm going to hit you. One, two..."

Keep in mind a concrete threat does not have to be verbal. A person could purposely move to block your exit, for example, or grab the phone and not let you make a call. She could physically make a specific sign, such as positioning her finger to look like it is pulling the trigger of a gun or is slitting a throat.

6. Has a Predisposition to Violence

A predisposition to violence should warn you not only that the person's threat needs to be taken *very* seriously but also that it can be a pretense for what he wanted from the beginning: to be violent. He wants to hurt you and making a threat provides the rationalization that he tried everything to get what he wanted—including warning you of the violence that is to come—and therefore now has the justification to harm you. He even threatens to hurt you knowing you cannot fulfill his demand—it might be absolutely unrealistic or unattainable—and again thereby justifies to himself that at least he warned you. Now when you fail to act positively in response to his threat he can aggressively act on it. This type of warning is even more dangerous when the person derives a sadistic pleasure from your fearful anticipation of his acting on the threat. "You should have known better than to doubt me. Now I have to hurt you!"

A group of my friends who play various sports in the park each weekend were unable to play one time when another group was already in our usual space. One of our players, a very athletic and strong man, walked up to them and told them that they had to leave and if they had a problem with it they would have to "take me on." They said they were there first and he had no right to threaten them, but when he did not capitulate and they saw he was serious, they departed. I had no doubt that the man in our sports group would not have been disappointed if the interlopers had chosen to ignore his warning and "taken him on."

Danger is particularly imminent if you know the threatening person has a history of violence. A violent past is one of the key predictors of violence. This is compounded if the person was also a victim of violence (e.g., being abused as a child or having been in a situation that resulted in post-traumatic stress disorder). It is also helpful to know whether the person's violence was committed in the distant or recent past. If the violence was a relatively long time ago, he might have changed and become less aggressive, but recent violence creates a greater likelihood that the person might be more inclined to act on his threat. Also, it is good to know if the violence was a single event or repeated events. Acting on a threat is a greater likelihood if the person has had multiple violent occurrences. A single event might have been a one-time experience while repeated events suggest the person is prone to violence. If Bonnie had known about Tom's history of violence—had she personally known it or read it in his charts—then she would have more seriously believed his threat that he would hurt her if he did not get his medicine.

7. Disregards Warnings

Another significant sign that a threat is leading to violence is when you warn the person of severe consequences for her threatening behavior and your warning is met with disregard or disdain. This person is so committed to acting on her threat that she is impervious to its negative repercussion. She does not care if the police are called or if anything bad happens to her. She lacks the normal fears, such as worrying about going to jail, that inhibit most people acting on aggressive impulses. I had a client who had developed an "institutionalized" mentality: i.e., he had been accustomed to a recidivist life of being in and out of prison and so telling him that you were going to call the police in response to his threat resulted in the aggressive retort "Bring them on!"

Maybe it is not so much that the threatening person does not care about consequences of her behavior but rather does not think about them or assess their significance. Remember the earlier discussion about how an angry person is driven by emotions and so is less rational. She might not be receptive to—or even understand—a logical discussion about the ramifications of her threat. She might not be in an emotionally stable state and so does not respond with equanimity to your logical explanation of what would happen if she were violent. Maybe she was originally somewhat logical in attempting to make you do what she wanted, but when she fails in that task, she becomes more desperate and less rational about comprehending the consequences of her actions. She loses interest in talking about her situation or in what you think about it and will only talk about how you are going to acquiesce to her demands. Telling the person the repercussions of her threatening behavior does not necessarily make her think about what will happen and instead results in "So what" or "That's got nothing to do with what happens next!"

Couple this lack of concern for consequences with the same sentiments toward social mores, such as it being wrong to hurt someone. Add the possibility that the person does not care about what happens to you if she hurts you and the danger of violence grows exponentially.

8. Is Under the Influence of Alcohol or Drugs

The final indicator that a threat should be considered dangerous is when a person is either under the influence of drugs/alcohol—"I wouldn't have done it if I hadn't drank so much"—or expresses paranoid thinking: "I know you're out to get me!"

You need to be watchful for the presence of any of these signs that indicate a threatening person could potentially become violent. Missing or misreading them can get you hurt. But do not always count on signs, on belligerent body language or on a blatant disregard for consequences to consider whether to take a threat seriously. It is always best to be vigilant any time you are threatened. It is good to listen to your gut, to the fear or to the suspicion that "something bad is going to happen." These feelings—along with the above indicators—should mobilize you to respond quickly and decisively to defuse the threatening situation before you are hurt.

Defuse Threatening Anger

You have assessed a person's threat to be real because of the presence of one or more of the warning signs, so what do you do to defuse it before you become a victim of violence? This possibility of violence makes it easy to overreact to a person's threat. Not many of us have had encounters with actual threats of harm and such inexperience makes us susceptible to becoming overly aggressive or even panicking when confronted with it. Contributing to this response is that a threat causes your body to instinctually shift into the earlier examined fight/flight defensive reaction. While protecting yourself is important, responding aggressively to a threat can have the opposite, unintended effect of pushing the person to act on his threat.

What do you do when threatened that will prevent your over-reacting and at the same time contribute to protecting you from the threat? Especially important in this stage is to stay calm. It is important to maintain your composure so you do not panic or rush to act on adrenaline and instead can calmly assess the degree of danger and wisely choose the appropriate intervention to defuse that danger.

For example, a person who threatens to stab you is very scary, easily causing you to overreact or even panic. You immediately want to ensure your safety, but you need to do so by acting out of the composure that helps you better assess the situation before you respond. You do not want to act on your instinct to grab the person's knife, which could result in your getting stabbed, before first determining if there are less risky means to defuse the situation. Also, you might not want to act on the impulse to call the police when doing so can push the person to cut you before the police arrive. Maybe the person has no intention to use the knife and only wields it to scare you. These are some of the questions you want to answer before you decide what to do and which are easier to answer when they arise from a calm rather than anxious response to the person's threat.

You can help yourself remain calm by reminding yourself that while a threat is dangerous it also means the person is *considering* violence and is not at that moment *committed* to it. If he really wanted to hurt you he probably would have hurt you already rather than threaten you and so he still possesses some restraint. You have not yet lost him to violence. Remind yourself that his goal is not to hurt you and instead is to get what he wants; your goal is to show him you want to work with that part of him that is willing to resolve his problem without violence. It is the part of him that threatens *in order not* to have to be violent and which warns so as to find a solution before it is too late and he is compelled to act on what he warned.

How do you work with this side of the threatening person that is not committed to becoming violent? Maybe you would rather read about how to protect yourself against that side of the person that might act on the threat and hurt you. This is reasonable since

it involves your safety. The next chapter will examine how to protect
yourself if the person actually tries to hurt you but the following
pages will help you be able to defuse the person's threat so he does
not become violent.

Be Prepared

Your first response to a person's threat—after staying calm and
assessing the seriousness of the threat—is to prepare yourself for
the possibility that you will not be able to defuse his threat and he
becomes violent. Examine the area around you and take note of
what can be used as a weapon, such as a lamp that might be thrown
at you. If you are in an office, make sure there are no objects on
your desk that can be used to hurt you, such as scissors. Inconspic-
uously remove any such objects if they are present or unobtrusively
move the person away from them.

If possible stand with your back to an exit. Make sure you
have access to escape routes: note doors or windows and make sure
the angry person is not impeding the way to them. In a similar
manner, the angry person needs to feel you do not have him stuck
in a corner. In spite of his threatening bravado, and maybe because
of it, he knows he may need to flee and if you are in front of the
exit he will feel anxious and act more aggressively toward you in
order to make his escape possible. The frequently discussed client
Tom never moved from standing directly in front of the receptionist's desk, knowing that if he hit the receptionist he would then need
to quickly exit through the front door. Bonnie was seated behind
the desk and she too needed to become aware of routes for escape
when she was threatened.

Do your best to make sure the person is always in front of you.
Being able to observe his facial expressions and intensity of eye contact can alert you to his intentions. It also allows you to note physical
movements, such as what he is doing with his hands: is he aggressively
shaping them into fists or are they holding/hiding something that can
be a weapon? Be attentive to what he is wearing: baggy clothes or a
coat can conceal something that could be used to hurt you.

Note the effect on the person from other people in the vicinity. Do they inhibit his aggressiveness, as if shaming him should he become violent, or do they exert peer pressure to act on his threat due to the fear of "losing face" should he back down? If the latter, you want to move the person away from others, but do not, as a result, be alone with him: that would be extremely pernicious. You are less vulnerable remaining with others. If you are in a professional situation and removing the person from your office or reception area is not working (e.g., he refuses to leave) and you feel it will not escalate the person if you call for help, then call. (If your work situation is one which typically encounters potentially violent people, such as an emergency room or clinic, consider having a sign on the wall that states your work place policy has a zero tolerance for violence: this can be a small but helpful deterrent in that it makes the person think about the prohibition on violence.)

In any threatening situation, do not wait until the threat turns into violence before you call for help. Even if part of you feels embarrassed to ask for assistance, as if acknowledging you cannot deal with the situation on your own, tell yourself it is critical to call for help. Others can provide needed support and might have more experience with this type of situation. They also can bring with them a visible "show of force" that lets the threatening person know you are in control. So tell the person you want to help her but that it is beyond your level of expertise and you will call someone such as a supervisor or co-worker. "I can't do this on my own, so let's get my boss who can give you the help you need."

You should have a system in your workplace where you use a coded phrase to alert others to get help for situations when you think calling someone for assistance will make the threatening person suspicious and therefore quickly act on his threat before help arrives. For example, if the coded phrase is "I'll be late for my next appointment," tell the angry person "I need to call the receptionist to tell her I'll be late for my next appointment" and do so in order for her to send help immediately.

Be careful, however, when you call for help because bringing someone into the situation can make the angry person feel attacked or cornered and thereby escalate her aggression. Some people, on the other hand, might enjoy the extra attention and feel further stimulated by it. Also keep in mind that when you get help from others you should have only one person lead the communication with the person. Otherwise he might feel you are ganging up on him and he will react aggressively.

Let the threatening person know what you are doing so he will not be suspicious. If you are leaving the room for a moment, tell the person and give a time frame for your return. If you are calling a supervisor or co-worker for help, tell her so she does not think you are calling the police. Even make known seemingly simple actions, such as if you are about to sit down, saying, "I am just going to sit here for a moment." In this way the person will not be surprised by a sudden movement or by your walking away unannounced—perhaps thinking you are leaving to call the police—thereby prompting her possible move to hurt you before you have a chance to leave.

If you need to exit the room because no help is forthcoming and you are afraid to be alone with the threatening person, do so only as a last resort to protect yourself from his possible acting on his threat. You might think it better to leave than to stay alone with the threatening person, but it is dangerous to simply walk away. It can make you appear frightened or vulnerable, as well as be insulting to the person or a danger to him, because he thinks you might be going to the police, thus compelling him to pursue you and hurt you or at least physically prevent your exit. Remember that turning your back while walking away can make you an easy target. So do not walk away unless, as we shall see in the next chapter, you are about to be hurt and you have no other choice.

Do Not Threaten Back

The first approach to defusing the threatening person, after staying calm and assessing the situation, is not what you do but what you do *not* do: do not aggressively challenge him. To disengage threatening behavior do not threaten back. This is counterintuitive to earlier discussed self-protective instincts. If someone stands up to threaten you then viscerally you feel the need to stand up to do whatever it takes to stop his threat. Yes, you need to do whatever it takes to stop the threat but know that an aggressive response usually does not succeed and instead likely pushes the person into violently acting on his threat. Remember that the person has warned you of harm and any excuse—such as your becoming aggressive in response—can serve to rationalize his assaulting you. He feels powerful scaring you with his threat and so challenging him—"You're going to do what to me?"—or trying to undermine his threat—"Go ahead and try!"—threatens that power. Movie heroes' aggressive responses silence the villains' threats, but in real life they usually make the person feel he has been pushed into a corner and has to act on his threat in order to maintain his power.

Telling the threatening person, "You better not be threatening me" usually will *not* be met with, "You're right, sorry" and instead with, "What are you going to do about it?" Now you have to do something, which challenges him to follow through on his threat before you follow through on yours. What once was a threat intended to force your acquiescence now escalates into a power struggle in which the person feels forced to act on his threat to show it is real. You will lose that contest, because he will not accept defeat and instead will "up the ante" by acting on his threat. "I warned you what I would do and now you've forced my hand!"

Remember the earlier stage example of Carol, an angry person who said, "You make me so angry I feel like I could break this lamp!" That was not a threat, but saying, "I am going to break this lamp unless…" now makes it one. If you say, "You better not be threatening me" or "Break the lamp; see what happens", your challenge will probably escalate the threat. Instead of the person responding, "Oh, okay; I'll put the lamp down", you have forced the person into a corner where she feels she has to break the lamp. "Oh yeah? Just watch me!" Or more critically she threatens to break the lamp on you. At least when she was simply threatening to break the lamp—and even if she broke it—it was not you that was in imminent danger. It was an inanimate object. Now your challenge escalates the power struggle and it *is* you who is in danger. She is going to throw the lamp at you and in response you possibly warn her, "Break the lamp and I will call the police." She probably will not back down, because you have not given her an "out." Now you have to call the police. Calling the police will further escalate the person's anger, possibly resulting in her throwing the lamp at you and fleeing before the police arrive.

Not challenging the threatening person does not mean accepting her threatening behavior. She might break the lamp if you do nothing to let her know it is unacceptable. Threats require a concise intervention that sets firm although non-confrontational limits that clearly let the person know threats will not be tolerated. "Threatening me does not help solve your problem, so I need you to stop it and let's figure out how to help you." Tell the person you understand: "I know you mean what you're saying…" and at the same time let him hear you will not tolerate it: "…and I also know you want this problem solved, so you need to stop the threats and let's work on it."

Think of the earlier example of Tom who argued with the receptionist about not getting his medicine until in desperation he said he better see the doctor in ten seconds or he would hurt someone. After reminding herself to stay calm and also after assessing whether Tom might act on his threat and how to protect herself if he does, Bonnie should have not challenged him and should have confidently let him know she was in control of the situation. Rather than saying, "Keep counting like that and I will call the police," which would have exacerbated the crisis, she could have firmly said, "I want to help, but I don't respond well to threats so let's stop that and I'll call the doctor to see if anything can be done." Or, "I can see you're angry, but it's not okay to threaten me. So stop the threats and let's see what we can do to help you."

The same can be said of the earlier example Susie who became defensively angry and then became hostile in response to the insensitivity of her husband. Her anger was meant to push Derrick away but when he continued to insist on talking about her anger Susie became exasperated and finally told him, "Back off or I swear I will push you back." He responded, "See, that is what I am talking about—how crazy is it that you are threatening me?" Derrick did not realize *how* crazy it was as evidenced by his surprise when, not backing off from his insistence on getting her to talk about her anger in spite of her warning, Susie forcefully shoved him out of her way and walked out the door. She wanted her threat to be taken seriously, which he could have done while also addressing the threat by saying, "It's lousy you feel you have to threaten me, but that me makes me realize how serious you are and so I'll back off and you can stop threatening me."

Acknowledge Threat

Do you let the person know his threat frightens you? The answer is yes and no. Knowing you are afraid of his threat emboldens the person; it makes him think he successfully "got" to you and can force you to do what he wants. You do not want to encourage his threatening behavior with signs of being scared, but at the same time you want him to know you take his threat seriously.

Non-aggressively acknowledging a person's threat addresses its seriousness without validating its intent. You may recall an earlier statement we discussed about not addressing the *how* of a person's anger—in this case, the threat—and instead focusing on *what* angers the person. While that is true in earlier anger stages, in this threatening stage it is important to let the person know you are responding to his aggressive behavior. You do not want him to think you are ignoring the threat or taking it lightly and thereby making him more forcefully threaten you to ensure you understand. When he says, "Don't you realize I'm going to hurt you?", you do not want to act like it is nothing or you are oblivious to its consequences. Instead acknowledge it: "I can see you mean what you say." At the same time let him unequivocally hear you will not tolerate it: "I know you are serious, but I also know you want this problem solved, so you need to stop the threats and let's work on the problem." You can even directly acknowledge that the threat affects you while maintaining your composure. "I don't like being threatened just as you wouldn't, so let's stop the threats and concentrate on fixing the problem."

Melissa, a high school teacher, warned a student about his misbehavior. He refused to cease his inappropriate behavior and subsequently she gave the student detention. Melissa told me about being threatened by the student after assigning the detention. The student told Melissa, "You sign that detention form and it will be the last one you ever sign!" She did not respond to his threat and gave him the detention form. When she turned her back to walk away, the student stood up as if to attack her. He felt compelled to act on his threat at least in part because he made the threat in front of his schoolmates and so he had to save face, as well as to show his teacher that she could not disrespect him by ignoring his warning. Some other students stood protectively between the student and the teacher, after which security was summoned and the student was expelled.

Melissa told me she had been frightened to acknowledge the student's threat, because she thought it would make him think he had power over her and thereby would hurt her if she gave him the detention. After we talked about the situation, she realized she could have more effectively defused the volatile situation not by ignoring his threat but instead by directly addressing it with something like, "[Name of student], it's just a detention. You can handle it, but you're turning it into something more serious with your threat and you don't want to do that."

Acknowledging a person's threat has a further advantage in that it allows for the dialogue that might give you an insight into what the person is thinking or what kind of plan he has. Rather than aggressively responding to a threat with, "You are going to do what to me?", you can ask a non-confrontational question about what the person said in order to ascertain if there is a concrete plan behind the threat. "Come on; do you really mean that?" The result might be a welcome, "Did you hear a threat? I'm not threatening you!" If the person says he really means it and says *how* he means it, you know you have a dangerous situation.

Bryce, a client, told me he was going to hurt his social worker—one of my co-workers—if she did not "get off my case." I told him I had to take his threat seriously and asked him if he really meant it. He said no, that he felt upset because of the way she supposedly mistreated him, but he was only "spouting off" and would never hurt her. Judging from my earlier described checklist of threat assessment, I concluded his threat did not have a real risk of being acted on. I could make this conclusion because I directly talked with him about his threat and clarified what he meant by it rather than ignoring the threat. However, had he answered that he was seriously thinking of hurting his social worker, I would have had to tell him that I had to report it to the police and to my threatened co-worker (according to California's Tarasoff Act) and then do so.

Alternative Solutions

Acknowledging a person's threat makes him know you understand it without capitulating to it. He thereby might feel he has no recourse but to act on his threat to achieve what he wants. "I've had enough of your stalling and now you leave me no choice!" Let the person know he *has* other choices and *not* hurting you is one of them.

You want the person who threatens you to see he is not stuck in a situation where the only way to "save face" is to act on his threat. He needs an "out" that makes him feel he can back down from his threat without "losing face." "I know you can break that lamp if you want, but there has to be a better way to fix this problem." Help him realize he can escape from that corner without having to fight his way out and, at the same time, maintain his honor or self-esteem. "Come on; we all say things when we are angry that we really don't mean. Let's forget about it and stop with the threats so we can figure this out."

You have a critical situation if the person says he *does* mean what he threatened. Even then, however, give him an alternative to acting on his threat by letting him know it is not too late. Tell him there is still a way out of the crisis no matter how threatening he has been and that he has not reached "the point of no return." "I know what you said, but you have not done anything wrong, so let's figure out how to make this work." Giving the person this option is especially pertinent if a weapon is involved. "It's not too late to settle this problem. No one has been hurt, so let's put the gun away and resolve this." You might be thinking, *I am supposed to let him get away with pulling a gun on me?* I suggest to you that the fact he threatened you with a weapon is reprehensible, but at that moment all that is important is you get him not to act on his threat to use the weapon. Confront him later with the ramifications of his threat when you are safely out of harm's way.

Heidi, a social worker I know, was threatened by her client Frank, a man who demanded a hotel voucher after he got evicted from his place of residence. Heidi told him he was not eligible for one, to which the client said she was prejudiced and that is why she would not give him a voucher. When she told him it had nothing to do with being prejudiced, but she could not give him a voucher, Frank said he would hit her if that is what it would take to make her realize he needed a voucher.

The social worker commendably maintained her composure, applying to the volatile situation all the techniques addressed in these pages, such as listening attentively and telling the client she knew it was important to get a voucher but that he should not threaten her. He aggressively replied, "What are you going to do, call the police?" Heidi responded that she did not want to call the police but that he had to stop threatening her or she would have no choice but to call them. He replied, "Go ahead. Call the police. At least I'll have a place to sleep since you're not giving me a voucher." Heidi reminded Frank how much he would miss his girlfriend and hanging out with his friends if he were in jail and suggested he let her try to get him in a temporary shelter while she helped him apply for hotel eligibility. It was not an ideal solution, she acknowledged, but it was something that helped him and also kept the police away. Applying for eligibility and getting other forms of assistance was an alternative to acting on his threat, one he reluctantly chose and which thereby defused a potentially pernicious situation.

Establish Consequences

What if your alternatives are not accepted and even after you have made it clear that the person's threat is unacceptable her warning becomes more intense? Remember, a threat is likely to lead to violence if it increases in intensity. "I've had enough of your talk—just give me it or I *will* hurt you!" It is time to change your approach when your attempt to defuse a person's threat is met with more aggressive and menacing behavior. Your final option, after everything else fails, is to warn the person of the consequences of her threat. Telling her the repercussions for her actions might get her not to act on her threat. However, it *is* confrontational to tell someone you are calling the police or feels punitive when you say you are terminating services because of the person's threat—thereby likely causing an even more aggressive reaction—and that is why it is something you do only as a last resort. Warning a person about repercussions should be done in a way that minimizes the likelihood of the warning coming across as being confrontational and especially punitive.

Rather than saying, for example, "You'll go to jail if you do that," get the person to *think* about consequences. Remember, there are social prohibitions against violence and something has stopped the threatening person from thinking about them or at least thinking about them thoroughly; you want him to reconsider his threat in the light of thinking about what will happen if he acts on his threat. "I know you are really angry, but think about what you are saying." This response to a threatening person does not come across as confrontational and instead might actually get him to think about what he is doing. The result of thinking about his behavior might help him realize that the repercussions of his actions outweigh the benefits he derives from threatening you. He will back down from his threat if he concludes the cost of his action is too high. "I can see you are serious, but ask yourself if it's really worth going to prison. There has to be a better way." However, he might be unfazed by your bringing the law into the situation. "I don't care about going to jail!" You can still maintain a non-confrontational stance and get him to reconsider the repercussions by telling him, "You might not care now, but you will later in jail, so let's work this out without any police getting involved."

My friend Jan asked me what she should do when her boyfriend threatened her. I told her to leave the relationship before she was hurt. Unfortunately, like many victims of domestic violence, she had numerous practical reasons for not leaving (e.g., he was enrolled in anger management classes and they were in couples counseling) as well as deeper psychological reasons for not leaving him (e.g., the fear of being alone outweighing the fear of being hurt). Jan would put up with no talk of leaving the relationship and simply wanted to know the most effective way to defuse his threats.

Reluctantly agreeing to set aside the obvious discussion of leaving him, I began to tell her about the typical violent partner. She interrupted to correct me, stating her boyfriend had never been violent and had only threatened to be. I amended my statement and continued to tell her that a threatening partner exerts control over the woman via his threat. It frightens the woman, making her compliant to the man's needs and thus reaffirming his control. Over time the fear of his violence takes deep root and makes the victim timid and afraid, not only of him but also of life in general. This renders her even more compliant to the man's control for fear of being on her own. If Jan was going to minimize the possibility of her boyfriend's hitting her as he threatened, she needed to let him feel in control *and*, if she was not going to shrink in fear of him or of life, she had to simultaneously stand up for herself. "I know what you are saying is important to you, but I also need you to know that threatening me is going to wind up with one of us in jail and neither of us want that, so we need to find another way to work out this problem." The boyfriend probably would not let the possibility of jail interfere with his compulsion to threaten his girlfriend. Jan would eventually have to leave him or be hurt by him.

Shaun, a client, told me of how he could no longer tolerate the emotional abuse he took from the manager of his apartment building. He had decided he was going outside to sit in his car and wait for her to leave the building, at which point he would drive his car into her. Not giving me the opportunity to ask questions to ascertain if his threat was serious, I followed him outside to his car and told him that I had to contact the police to prevent him from hurting or possibly killing the apartment building manager. Shaun said he did not care, that he had to do what he had to do and I had to do what I had to do. I called the police on my cell phone so Shaun could see what I was doing and as a result he drove away before the police or the manager appeared.

Deal with Threatening Behavior

First, clearly let the threatening person know the repercussions of her actions. Ambiguous communication is more likely to encourage the belief she can get what she wants by threatening violence. You warned the person she *might* be terminated from your program for threatening you and, after continuing to threaten you, she responds to your warning by saying, "You never said you would kick me out!" Another person is not convinced by your warning, because she has seen others "get away with it" or did not think you were serious. Be clear in communicating consequences.

Second, not all threats are premised on physical violence. A mean boss may threaten his workers with loss of employment. Another person might warn her partner that she will leave him if he does not comply with her demands, knowing her partner is plagued by abandonment anxiety and so will do whatever it takes to prevent her departure. A belligerent customer who does not receive what he feels he is entitled to receiving may threaten the store clerk with going to the clerk's supervisor and ensuring that the clerk loses his job. While these are not physical threats, they need to be taken seriously and require similar interventions as examined in these pages.

Third, do not panic—even if the person threatens you with a weapon. Remind yourself he has not immediately used it, which he would have done if he was simply being punitive, so you still have time to negotiate with him. Negotiation should be centered on the person's need to feel in control and a weapon makes him feel less vulnerable and more in control. "You better do it or I'm going to introduce you to my shotgun!"

The first rule when a person has a weapon is not to do anything foolish or seemingly heroic. Do not think you are in a movie where you can grab the weapon out of the angry person's hand. And do not say anything inflammatory ("You don't have the guts to use it") or challenging ("I'm calling the police").

The second rule is to do your best to keep the person calm. "I want to help you, but guns make me very uncomfortable. Can you please put it away so we can work at this calmly?" You have a concession if he agrees to put the gun away and now can negotiate further. If he refuses, ask him at least to put the gun on the floor or on the table so no one gets accidently hurt. This still allows him close enough proximity to the weapon to feel in control while you have put some distance between the threat and hastily acting on it. Now you have some space to continue trying to defuse the situation.

A client named Dave told me he had a gun, patting his pocket where I could see its outline. Dave said he would use it if needed. I told him I knew he would use the gun, which made him know I took him seriously, and then I established boundaries: "I will do all I can to help you and all I ask is you keep the gun in your pocket. Okay?" Dave never displayed his gun, satisfied that he had not only my undivided attention but also my non-confrontational expectation that he would sensibly keep the gun in his pocket if I did all I could to help him.

My client kept his gun at a distance, but another person might not respect your similarly sensible negotiations and instead more aggressively threaten you with his gun. Do not argue with him and try to keep him talking. This will hopefully keep him engaged with you and less prone to act on his threat. It will also give you time to further assess the situation so as to determine how to protect yourself if the person tries to hurt you.

Fourth, if you cannot defuse a person's threat and your only choice is to comply with his demands or be hurt, then comply. You might feel like you are giving in or rewarding him for threatening behavior but, when all else fails, your primary concern is your safety. You need to do whatever it takes not to be harmed (as well as for others in your vicinity not to be hurt by the angry person's actions). So give the person what he wants if it is in your power. I told Heidi, the social worker who commendably defused the man who threatened to hurt her if she did not give him a hotel voucher, that had there been no resolution to this crisis except that of giving him the voucher—even though he was not entitled to it—then her only option would have been to give it to him and to deal with the consequences later. It was not worth her getting hurt.

Fifth, do not assume the worst is over even if you give in to the threatening person's demands. Your acquiescence to his threat can make you appear compliant and make him hit you because you are weak and gave in to his demand. I have seen this in domestic violence situations where one person did everything her partner demanded and he still hit her, because it made her appear weak and he could not tolerate weakness. Or the anger and aggressiveness underlying a person's threat is so compelling that he acts on his threat— even though you acceded to his demands—simply to be punitive. Another possible outcome as it pertains to Heidi's situation could have been that she gave the hotel voucher to the threatening client, because he had been unrelenting in his threat to hurt her and then he hit her, believing he felt she humiliated him by originally not giving him the voucher and making him beg for what in his mind should have been rightly his. Be vigilant in these and all situations involving threats.

If the person is going to hurt you regardless of whether you accede to his demands, because he does not care about consequences or he feels he has no choice but to hit you to get what he wants, then you have entered the final stage of violence and your next step is to protect yourself. Before examining that, however, we will briefly discuss three categories of people—sociopaths, psychotics and people under the influence of drugs/alcohol—whose anger and threats need to be taken particularly seriously.

Sociopathy

The sociopathic personality, unlike most people who become angry when they are frustrated with a situation, possesses a deeply ingrained predisposition to approaching problems by resorting to threats and violence in order to resolve them. Most of us do not count sociopaths among our acquaintances, but we sometimes encounter them at work or in social settings. While we are usually at a loss to say exactly what it is about them, we know there is something unusual and a little unnerving about how they present themselves. Usually that is because these sociopaths—the majority are males—might appear self-assured and passionate about who they are but we quickly become privy to a darker side of them that shows them to be antisocial, manipulative, vengeful, pathological prevaricators and generally lacking regard both for others and for the consequences of their actions. They aggressively turn relationships into "either you are with me or against me" and see the world as filled with "givers and takers", with the sociopaths being takers with the right to forcefully take from you that which you do not give them. They probably also possess psychopathic qualities, which generally refer to internal psychological dynamics such as being unemotional, paranoid, aggressively impulsive and possessing an inflated sense of superiority.

My neighbor Keith came to me for advice or at least I thought he was seeking my advice. Rather, it was what he considered a mutually beneficial encounter in which he tried to convince me to side with him in changing the way our condominium's homeowners' association was enforcing rules. Keith believed the association members were transgressing regulations and that they had singled him out, because he stood up to them. He wanted to know if I would join with him to take the association members out of power and restore a rightful democratic process. When I did not immediately agree with his assessment, he turned on me. "I thought you were different and instead you're just like them! I'm warning you that when I take them down you will fall with them unless you join me!"

When you combine the internal psychological characteristics of the sociopath—such as my neighbor's paranoia and impulsivity—with external antisocial traits—such as manipulation and aggressively threatening behavior—you have several reasons to take this person's threat very seriously.

First, the sociopath has no morals or guilt and so does not think it is wrong for *him* to do whatever it takes to get what he wants, including violence. Hence telling him it is unacceptable to threaten you is meaningless, because he does not perceive anything wrong with threatening you: it is simply the way to get what he needs or wants. What is wrong is his being denied something. Add to this his belief that nothing good comes to him by waiting and so he impulsively wants any problem—no matter how intractable—fixed *now*.

Second, you will have a difficult time trying to convince the angry sociopath not to act on his threat. You cannot reason with him, because he has no insight into what makes him do what he does and because his grandiosity makes him absolutely right and you wrong. Keith, for example, quickly dismissed any legitimate concerns I introduced in response to his harangue against our homeowners' association. Further, you will have grave difficulty persuading the sociopath against acting on his threat, because you cannot appeal to the part of him that might be concerned if he hurt you since he has no capacity for the empathy that would bother him if he did harm you and which normally inhibits people's violent tendencies. Nor can you appeal to consequences (such as calling the police) that also inhibit violent tendencies since he is not swayed by consequences. "Go ahead; call the police!"

Third, the sociopath initially might not appear angry when he demands something, instead getting his way by seductively conning people. His charm, however, is only to achieve a goal and he becomes angry and potentially violent if you're not taken in by it.

Fourth, the sociopath trusts nobody. He will not form a collaborative relationship with you in order to work on resolving his problem, because he does not trust your intentions. If he forms a relationship with you—as did my neighbor—he does so only to further his cause and still does not trust you. His inability to trust also makes him pathologically distort the truth to get what he wants. A man I know did not like the director of a program to which he belonged and he manipulated every possible situation to sabotage the woman's leadership. He gathered people together who were sympathetic to his cause and conflated their worries into a witch hunt, getting them to sign petitions and demand her resignation. He even subsequently met with the director, his adversary, to warn her about the conspiratorial group, thereby making her unsuspicious of his involvement in the plot to overthrow her.

Fifth, the sociopath is a sensation seeker. He is bored easily and so craves the adrenaline rush of antisocial behavior. While other aggressive people attempt to provoke you into escalating a crisis so as to have an excuse to become violent, he does not need an excuse: he will hurt you "for the fun of it."

Sixth, the sociopath enjoys frightening you. Sometimes the sociopath is not even interested in solving his problem and mostly is motivated by scaring you. He likes being perceived as dangerous. He takes a sadistic pleasure in the pain he threatens as well as in the pain he delivers. I counseled a sociopath who warned me he would "have my job" when I did not agree with his assessments; he meant it and worked at making it happen.

Finally, the sociopath is particularly pernicious, because often he does not display the earlier discussed warning signs of mounting anxiety and anger leading to an emotional explosion. You do not see this underlying anger, because he is always in control. As a result he unexpectedly threatens you with "cold–blooded" vengeance, making you the victim of his motto "Do not get angry; get even!" The absence of mounting tension leading toward violence means you will probably be unprepared to protect yourself when the violence comes.

Defuse the Sociopath

Even before you try to defuse the sociopath's threat you must prepare yourself for the possibility of violence, because in the end, it is the ultimate answer to whatever it is that upsets him. You want to try to defuse his threat before it escalates into violence and so employ the various approaches to defusing threats discussed in this chapter. Here are a few more ideas on de-escalation that might be of particular help in dissuading the sociopath from acting on his threat.

The most important insight into the sociopath is that he unequivocally needs to be in control. You, at any cost, must not relinquish your control. You need to stand your ground, because otherwise the sociopath will see you as either weak or aggressively overreacting. Either way, he knows he has "gotten to you." You instead want him to know you have not been "gotten." You need to stand up to him, but in doing so make it clear that you're not looking to fight or to control him and instead are standing up to him because you are in control of your own life. Being confident but not confrontational helps him see you less as an enemy and more as an equal, if not someone to begrudgingly respect.

Staying calm and not overreacting will take away some of the adrenaline-driven drama that motivates sociopaths to threaten violence. They want you to cower in fear or aggressively react. The latter gives the sociopath an excuse to turn a crisis into a conquest. He "carries a chip on his shoulder" waiting for you to knock it off so he can knock you off. He thereby will have succeeded in pulling you into an altercation and he will win, because he has nothing to lose and, unlike some of the earlier discussed angry people, he will not back down.

Do not aggressively confront the sociopath. It will have the opposite effect of de-escalation. Warning him of consequences, remember, is of no concern to him since he is not future oriented and instead is compelled by immediate gratification. He becomes violent in spite of—and maybe in part because of—your warning of consequences. (He will also possibly become violent repeatedly, because sociopaths do not learn from behavior that gets them in trouble; they do it again and when caught are jailed and often become habitual offenders.)

Confronting the sociopath will also exacerbate his anger because he hates people telling him what he can and, especially, cannot do. He does not have to abide by your rules since he is superior and rules are not meant for him. Telling him what to do also makes you appear as if you are saying you are right and he is wrong, when he thinks he is right and he does not care what anyone else thinks. He will not be denied his rightness and will do whatever it takes to prove he is right.

My neighbor's threat, for example, was his aggressive manner of telling me he was right and he would entertain no disagreement and that I had *better* know it. I clearly understood Keith's aggressive message and clarified my position that I did not disagree with what he was saying and rather that I understood his position. I also said I could see why it was important that he make his position known, which made him feel I was not threatening the control he exerted by standing up for himself. Now that I did not pose a threat to his control, I felt I could acknowledge that he had the courage to get his point across while also suggesting he could do it without necessarily including threatening language and thereby might be more successful in his plan. This flattered Keith's sense of superiority and helped him to see that his threatening behavior was not going to work with me.

Be attentive to the sociopath, therefore, such as my telling my neighbor that I would not be threatened while simultaneously flattering his sense of superiority. You thereby make the sociopath think nothing else matters except trying to help him resolve what makes him angry. Remember, nothing else matters, because your safety is at risk.

Psychosis

A sociopath's threat is scary but is not as unnerving as "God told me to kill you if you don't do as I say!" Previously discussed means of defusing threats have fewer efficacies when it comes to responding to a psychotic person's command hallucinations.

Psychosis is an illness characterized by disorganized and irrational thinking, hallucinations, feeling out of control and, at times, being out of touch with reality. These characteristics do not in themselves make a person violent. They can contribute to acting violently when they combine with other factors such as not taking antipsychotic medications that mitigate violence-inducing hallucinations. Do not presume that because a person hears voices he is dangerous. He can hear aggressive voices in his head but not feel compelled to act on them. The possibility of violence increases, however, when he not only has hallucinations but also feels agitated or disorganized and thereby less able to cope with everything going on around him.

Chloe, for example, takes antipsychotic medications that work wonderfully to diminish the voices in her head, but sometimes have no positive effect on helping her keep her thoughts in order. One thought intrudes on another, often conflicting with other thoughts and becomes irrational, which can cause her to feel out of control and even overwhelmed. She becomes confused when this happens and easily agitated, with the result being she aggressively yells at people who "make no sense" when talking to her. "Stop asking me questions—you're driving me crazy!"

The psychotic person's irrational and disorganized thinking makes it challenging to talk with her. Do not be surprised when she does not respond rationally to your attempt to get her to think about consequences or find logical solutions to what angers her. Combine this with a psychotic person who is also paranoid and you have a significant challenge to de-escalating her anger. The paranoid person does not trust you and suspects you are "out to get him" or are trying to control his life. This can make him misinterpret an innocuous event—e.g., thinking you are talking about him when you are only talking in general—and result in his thinking you are persecuting him. "I'm going to make you stop controlling me!" "I can't take your doing this to me anymore!"

A psychotic woman was on the roof of her apartment building threatening to drop cement blocks on the street below. Several people told her she would hurt someone and that the police had been called.

Unfazed by these warnings, she dropped a cement block off the roof. I suggested to her that something must be bothering her to make her drop the blocks, to which she said she warned everyone to get out of her way. I asked her if there was another means to get people out of her way, because it seemed like a huge effort to throw blocks off the roof. She suggested we move the blocks to the other side of the roof. We moved them—even though for no logical reason—and she stopped throwing the blocks off the roof.

Defuse the Psychotic

Try to keep the psychotic person focused on concrete issues. This minimizes some of her disorganized thinking and bizarre thought processes. Saying, "What exactly can we do so you can get on top of this" will help direct her thinking and make her feel a little more in control. But she might have difficulty keeping the conversation concrete and as a result will likely become impatient with your attempt to bring her "back to reality." Do not, however, become impatient with her. Remember that her disorganized thinking makes it difficult to clearly express feelings; arguing with her about the way she is expressing herself will not only not change her mind but also further convince her you are trying to control her thought processes. That is why arguing with the woman throwing cement blocks off the roof about what she was doing would have had no effect on her behavior and instead would have made her more confused.

Consider another example in which I witnessed the interaction between Henry, a psychotic person whose television set was turned on very loud, and Cindy, a social worker who argued with him about turning down the volume. I intervened when Henry threatened to hurt Cindy when she attempted to turn the volume down herself. We talked about why he liked the volume loud. He was not forthcoming at first, but when he realized I was not ordering him to turn the volume down, he gradually revealed he was not taking his medications and lately had been hearing voices to hurt someone. He played the television loudly to "drive out the voices." Forcing Henry to turn down the volume thereby would have had a deleterious effect, because it could have resulted in his hearing the voices and feeling overwhelmed by their aggressive commands. Arguing with him about turning the volume down made him more agitated and threatening. "You better stop telling me what to do if you know what's good for you!"

Defusing Henry's threat came from letting him tell us what was happening—as illogical as it may seem—rather than us telling him. Gradually Cindy and I were able to understand his situation and convince him we could help him with the voices by getting him back on his medication. In the meantime, he agreed to lower the volume of the television sufficiently so as to not disturb others while maintaining enough sound to silence the inner voices.

Not arguing with Henry, as with any psychotic person, did not mean indulging his hallucination or even agreeing with it. You do not want to respond to a person's hallucination as if it is real, though at the same time you must be careful not to dismiss it or "talk down" to the person about it for she will become even more distrustful of you.

Jane, a client of mine who is psychotic, told me that the rocks in her garden were demons and they warned her that the person in the next building was dangerous. She carried a bat as a result and threatened her neighbor with it when she was under the influence of her demon rocks. She asked me if I could see the demons, to which I replied that I did not see what she saw but that there obviously was a problem if what she heard was telling her to hurt her neighbors. My response did not indulge her hallucination and also did not make her think I was trying to convince her that the stones were simply stones and that the voices were hallucinations. The latter would have had no effect on her paranoia. Just the opposite. It would have made her think I was part of the dangerous conspiracy. She would have replied, "Of course you would say that—you're with them!"

I neither agreed nor disagreed with Jane's hallucination. I instead let her know I heard what she was saying, which I did by addressing her feelings rather than her irrational thought processes. "I don't know what you're hearing, but it seems to have gotten you real angry." This helped me connect with Jane on a common ground of reality, such as what she was feeling, which was real, even if her thoughts were illogical. In this way I was able to get her to talk about her feelings rather than act on her paranoia-fueled threat. When talking to a paranoid person like Jane, be sure that your body language does not betray your incredulity, such as a critical frown or a wink of an eye to another person.

Do not question the paranoid person too much. She will feel you are judging her or are trying to gather information to control her. Also, do not be evasive in what you say; be transparent so she has less reason to be suspicious of you. If you are not getting through to the person and fear she is going to act on her threat to become violent, you need to protect yourself.

Always try to ascertain if the psychotic person is not taking her prescribed medication or is on street drugs. The latter is a typical means of "self-medication", as we shall discuss in the next section. Either of these situations multiplies the risk of violence, especially if the normal dose of psychotropic medications is what keeps her calm and the streets drugs have her "amped up."

Tim, for example, was diagnosed as being bipolar. He was prescribed a medication to temper his extreme mood swings from depression to mania. However, he frequently did not take his medication, because while it "took the edge off" his manic behavior it also made him emotionally flat and easily bored. So he either did not take his prescribed medication or he supplemented it with drugs he bought on the street, which gave him the energy to "keep going all night."

However, while the street drugs gave him energy, they, along with the abandonment of his prescribed medication, also contributed to making him feel agitated, anxious, impatient and manic. While with friends Tim was often filled with an exorbitant amount of energy and aggressively pressured them to go out with him in the middle of the night even though they refused. Whenever they tried to persuade him not to go out (recognizing Tim's manic state and knowing the trouble it could cause him), he warned them not to try to prevent his going out on his own. "You might be ready for retirement but don't dare stand in the way of me having fun!"

Tim's friends learned that trying to stop him in his manic state was not only fruitless but also caused more agitation. Saying, "You seem wound up. Are you on anything?" made him angry. "What, you have to be on something to have fun? Get away from me if you think you are going to wreck my buzz!"

Inquiring about a person's drug intake can make someone like Tim feel controlled. It can also heighten other people's paranoia. "Why do you want to know? Do you think I'm crazy?" If that is the response you get when you try to ascertain if someone is on street drugs or is not taking prescribed psychiatric medicine, say, "Of course not. I am just concerned if you are having problems and I want to know if I can be of some help." If the person acknowledges not taking her medication or that she is taking street drugs then talk to her about the necessity of taking her medication or the negative effects of street drugs on her behavior. You will probably have to wait to have this conversation until a later time when she is not in a hyper-stimulated state because it makes her either belligerently unreceptive to or incapable of comprehending such a conversation.

There are some medications you should familiarize yourself with that help people with mental problems cope more effectively with aggressive impulses: antipsychotics are very helpful for organizing thoughts and ridding hallucinations; lithium helps bring down from the manic state and so lessens aggressive acting out and also helps modulate moods; antidepressants also are aids for impulse control, which sometimes lead to angry explosions; haloperidol is critical for rapid tranquilization in emergency rooms or clinics; anticonvulsants reduce the violent tendencies associated with organic brain damage.

Substance Abuse and Aggression

A final type of threat to consider is one that many of us have experienced or witnessed, which is made by a person under the influence of alcohol or drugs. Most people using drugs or alcohol are not typically violent. The potential for intense anger and even aggressive behavior exists when the person is under the influence of certain drugs or has consumed an excessive amount of alcohol. These intoxicants differ in their contribution to making people angry or threatening. We shall examine them separately before we discuss how to defuse a person under their influence.

Alcohol

Alcohol is commonly associated with aggressive behavior. It can be the culprit in everything from domestic disturbances to bar fights. Alcohol does not in itself make a person aggressive. It leads to aggressive behavior because it is a major disinhibitor of the psychological controls that normally constrain aggressive impulses. It begins as a low level stimulant, activating neurotransmitters in the brain that relaxes muscles and makes a person feel "no pain" and increasingly does so concomitant to the amount of alcohol consumed (until in the end it makes the person pass out or become depressed). But before the person "hits bottom", alcohol's loosening of restraints makes him more aggressive and less in control.

Combine this greater impulsivity with the cognitive impairment also caused by alcohol and it is understandable how a person becomes more aggressive. Alcohol consumption diminishes the rational functioning areas of the brain that make decisions and judgments, causing misperceptions of social cues which, in conjunction with disinhibitions, can make a person overreact aggressively to situations that otherwise might be handled with equanimity. Or it simply makes someone a "mean drunk."

A person drinking at a crowded bar, for example, is accidentally bumped and becomes angry as if the bump were deliberate. He pushes the person who bumped him back and threatens to hurt the person, even if the person is bigger. The person who was bumped acts recklessly, because alcohol impairs his judgment as well as loosens his control over aggressive impulses and finishes the one-two punch with an anesthetized-induced sense of not caring about external constraints or concerns for consequences (such as the harm done to others or the repercussions brought down on him, such as being hurt or arrested).

A further pernicious aspect of the disinhibiting effect of alcohol is that it makes the person feel she has a license to be reckless or irresponsible—"It was the liquor talking"—and so act on aggressive feelings she otherwise would be expected to control. "I know I shouldn't have hit him, but I was drunk."

An acquaintance named Greg is a classic case both of being a mean drunk and of being one who upon getting sober blames his meanness on the alcohol. He had an extraordinary amount of misfortune in his life that gave him ample reason to be angry. Greg managed to keep his anger under control until he drank alcohol, which he did often and excessively. The loosening of normative impulse control induced by the alcohol liberated the anger held deep inside him. The slightest provocation easily annoyed him and he subsequently became enraged when he misread the supposed provocateur's intentions, such as a person innocuously standing on the sidewalk presumed to be deliberately blocking his way. Should that person not get out of his way or should the person tell him to "sober up", Greg aggressively "got in his face" and threatened, "You better get out of my way if you know what is good for you!" Most people recognized the seriousness of this man's threat and so backed away when they saw him in his alcohol induced altered state, to which he said, "All right then" and continued on his way. Others did not back down, however, and altercations ensued. The next day, Greg blamed everything on the alcohol, including his inability to free himself of its control over making him aggressive.

Amphetamines and Cocaine

Speed and cocaine are highly popular drugs, because they increase energy and induce an exaggerated sense of power and physical strength. They do this by releasing dopamine from the brain, which gives the person the infamous "rush." At the same time, these drugs activate the adrenaline that increases blood pressure and over-stimulates the central nervous system. As a result, they can energize a person but also make him anxious, paranoid, hyperactive, impatient, irrational, irritable and, in extreme situations, exhibit psychotic symptoms. They furthermore can induce rapid mood swings from euphoria to agitation. All of these characteristics can easily lead to aggressive behavior.

When, for example, my friend's neighbor Rita gets high on crack (a form of cocaine that is processed into a small rock-like object that is burned and inhaled rather than snorted nasally), she becomes paranoid and believes that her other neighbor Don breaks into her apartment and steals her drugs. While this belief is the product of drug induced paranoia, it also has some basis in reality. Rita and Don use drugs together in Rita's apartment and so when she gets high and depletes her drug supply, her drug induced paranoia makes her think it is her drug-using neighbor who is stealing her drugs. She yells and threatens Don with her cane unless he gives back her "stash." Remember that a concrete weapon along with paranoia make the threat very serious.

Even more extreme are two clients, Eric and Sophia, whose intake of speed causes a drug induced psychosis that leads to threatening behavior. Eric sees a dangerous person outside his window—which due to its location is physically impossible—when he is high on methamphetamine. He does not recognize the person, but says he needs to find the person and kill him before the interloper sneaks in though the window and kills Eric. He has accused several people of being that intruder and has threatened to hurt them.

Sophia's excessive use of speed makes her feel bugs are crawling on her face, a common speed-induced hallucination. To her, the bugs are not merely a sensation and instead are real, causing her literally to try to scrape them off her face, resulting in horrible facial disfiguration. She subsequently becomes overly sensitive about people staring at her face—a fear in this case not based on paranoia but in reality since she truly disfigured her face and people sometimes are compelled to stare at her face. She subsequently warns them to stop staring.

A little less extreme is a person who, when high on cocaine, is energetic and amicable but who, when he comes down from that high, is depressed and easily provoked into anger and even threatening violence. People who know him can recognize his disposition by the sunglasses he wears when he is "down" and do what it takes to avoid triggering his intense anger. Those who do not know him unfortunately are unwittingly subject to his threats when they confront the inappropriateness of the angry behavior he exhibits toward them when withdrawing from his cocaine high.

Heroin and Opiates

Heroin and methadone are opiates. So too is oxycodone, which is a pain relieving prescription drug that has become very popular with street drug dealers and their clients. Opiates directly affect endorphins in the brain that make one feel good; when taken in the appropriate quantity, heroin and other opiates induce a plethora of endorphins that create a blissful state. A problem is that the opiate user's brain chemistry becomes dependent on the opiate and stops producing its own endorphins. The result is that when the opiate wears off and its feeling of well-being subsides, the person becomes depressed due to the lack of organic endorphins that would normally create feelings of well-being. The person who comes down from the high can become aggressively obsessed with the frantic need for the next fix, even threatening violence in order to "score" it.

My client Helen became addicted to heroin as a teenager. She had been terribly abused (physically and emotionally) as a child. She internalized that abuse into self-contempt, which expressed itself via feeling depressed and thoughts of hurting herself. Her initial experiment with heroin made her for the first time not hate or want to hurt herself. It was blissful. When the self-loathing returned after the heroin wore off, she even more intensely experienced her self-contempt and so sought more heroin for relief. It was the only time she felt free from her pain (using heroin for self-medication). So Helen sought the paradise of heroin frequently and equally frequently came the anguish of coming down from its high and again feeling miserable until "chasing Lady H" was what motivated her day. She had become addicted, unable to function without heroin. Helen was addicted both physically, in that her body achingly craved its chemical relief, and emotionally, in that she felt absolutely lost without its blissful absence of pain. The combination of the two was pernicious, compelling her to do whatever was necessary to score the next relief from pain. This included thievery and even threats to her family to give her money so she could buy more heroin.

Barbiturates are like heroin in that they can help calm an emotionally pained or anxious person. But also like heroin, they eventually wear off and the result is the person becomes agitated and angry. Although not generally associated with violence, sedatives' calming effect on a person lessens impulse control and as a result, under certain adverse situations, can make a person more aggressive.

Marijuana

Marijuana is not usually associated with aggression, although a high concentration of THC (the active ingredient in marijuana that makes a person high) can lead to aggressive behavior. Add PCP (phencyclidine) to marijuana, however, as is sometimes done for a more intense high, and the person is more likely to also experience paranoia, hallucinations and anxiety and is easily agitated to the point of violence. People who frequently use marijuana and who feel the absence of its high when not using it can find themselves feeling anxious during the "down" time.

Finally, inhalants can cause brain damage that leads to aggressive behavior and anabolic steroids, such as those taken for body building, can lead to intense anger ("roid rage").

Defuse Alcohol/Drug Induced Anger

How do you defuse the aggressive person who is on drugs or under the influence of alcohol? All the techniques described for previous stages of anger apply but with even greater vigilance. The angry person on drugs is even less rational and more impulsive than the angry person not on drugs. She is not going to be suddenly less under the influence of the drug's chemistry surging through her veins and compelling her to be aggressive simply because you talk with her or warn her of consequences of her behavior.Her ingestion of drugs or alcohol probably also means she might be sleep or nutritionally deprived and is more susceptible to being volatile. It requires great patience not to give up trying to de-escalate this person's drug induced anger.

The mean drunk is not going to respond positively to a conversation—and especially not to a stern lecture—about the inappropriateness of his threatening behavior. Helen, the woman who threatened her family for money to buy heroin, is not amenable to her family members' supportive suggestion that they do not want to contribute to her heroin habit by giving her money and she also aggressively warns them of what will happen if they do not give her money (e.g., she may go to jail if she is caught for burglary or she may contract AIDS from dirty needle use if she does not have the money for clean ones). A person coming down from his "coke high" is anxiously looking for anything in what people say to him as an excuse to blow up at them (and by doing so experience some temporary relief from his dreaded withdrawal).

The main approach to defusing the aggressive person on drugs/alcohol is to try to "talk her down." She is irrationally "all over the place" or is anxiously coming down from her high and as a result might feel out of control and agitated. Talking with her will help bring her "back to earth" and feel a little more "grounded." The more I talked with Eric, the man on methamphetamine who was threatening people he thought were trying to break through his window, the less he thought about the hallucinated person in the window and the paranoid fear the person elicited in him. It did not significantly matter what we talked about as long as I took his mind off the confusion he felt and the persecutory thoughts in his mind. He did not fully come down from his amped-up meth buzz, but he felt a little more grounded. In the midst of talking about nothing in particular, I asked him if he felt safe going back into his apartment. He said yes and returned to it. The threat to his neighbors was over. (It also helped him become less anxious, as it may for others who acknowledge drug use, when I let him know drugs were contributing to his agitation or to being out of control and that he would feel calmer when they wore off.)

Also remind yourself to stay calm, because it is easy to become frustrated when you tell an intoxicated person to stop yelling and she acts as if she does not hear you. You might have to repeat yourself several times in order for what you say to be understood by the person in an altered state. Talk with short and succinct statements, for the person who is under the influence of drugs will not be able to process long sentences. Repeat what you say until she comprehends it. Talk firmly, because the person's attention must be turned to you and to your attempt to get her to hear clearly what is problematic. "It's difficult talking with you when you're high."

Rita, the woman on crack, for instance, was pacing the hallway floor looking for the man who supposedly stole her drugs. Repeatedly beating her cane into her hand, she declared over and over, "Wait 'til I see him!" I talked firmly with her, hoping she would calm down. But she continued to pace and to pound the cane into her hand. I asked her to give me the cane, again hoping I had taken her mind off the alleged drug-stealing neighbor who was the target of her menacing cane. But she refused, holding the cane tighter and pounding it harder into her hand. I finally had to resort to warning her of consequences and telling her that the police would be called. I told her that while I understood her anger she did not want to be seen by the police wielding a cane in a threatening fashion. I reminded her of what it would be like in jail, without her apartment and her possessions in her apartment. In spite of her altered state she understood sufficiently what would happen to her if she continued her threatening behavior and so the next time I asked her for cane she reluctantly handed it to me and went back to her apartment.

Do not give up on the irrationally high person, like this woman on crack. She might hear something relevant to her situation and at least might find some reassurance in your calm and controlled manner. But be constantly vigilant, because intoxicants can make her unpredictable, whereby one moment she is passive or laughing and the next moment she is screaming or lunging at you. Get help or call the police if she is aggressively out of control and you cannot "bring her down." I would have had to call the police if I was unable to secure the cane from Rita. Otherwise someone's life could have been endangered.

While drugs or alcohol can make a person prone to anger and violence, the converse can also be true. Drugs/alcohol can be an escape from an anger that feels scary or unmanageable. A person can use drugs (those legally prescribed as well as street drugs) to self-medicate and to help control the underlying emotional pain or aggressive voices in her head that cannot otherwise be controlled. A vicious cycle ensues, however, when the person actively seeks situations that make her angry so she has an excuse to relapse back into the drugs/alcohol that soothe her. "It was terrible. If only I had a drink I could calm down." Anger provides the rationalization to use drugs and drugs complete the cycle by inducing an altered state in which the person is able to escape the anger—until sobriety returns and she again becomes angry.

The family members of Helen, who used heroin to vanquish painful memories and feelings, knew about this cycle of getting high, coming down from the high, finding excuses to get angry so as to have a reason to get high again. They knew all too well how she often came to their home in an originally calm state but then became agitated over a particular issue—real or imagined—and then demanded money from them for something she "needed", which they were aware was a pretense for scoring drugs. They learned to firmly say no; that though they understood her anxiety they would not indulge her habit. She usually stormed out of the house, threatening to come back and make them give her the money.

The same cycle transpired for Sophia, the woman who disfigured her face in reaction to the drug induced psychosis that her face was crawling with bugs. She had a cycle of stopping the use of speed and having her face begin to heal until she began craving the drug and intentionally created situations that upset her thereby providing the excuse to rid herself of the tension by returning to speed. She again aggressively disfigured her face. One time when I tried

to stop her, she not only threatened me if I prevented her from taking speed but also, even more agitated by what she did to her face
again, actually acted on her threat and this time became violent.

We now examine how to protect yourself from people whose
anger and threats—whether from drugs/alcohol, psychological
compulsions or learned aggressive behavior—cannot be defused
and instead climaxes in violence.

PROVIDE ALTERNATIVE OPTIONS

People who threaten you tend to believe acting on their threats is the only viable option to resolve the current conflict and get what they want. Other people *should* or *must* give in to their desires. However, there is an important distinction between demands and preferences:

- People *must* do what I tell them to do or things will be terrible.
- It would be *preferable* if people did what I wanted, but who am I to judge?

Help a person who threatens you to make this distinction. He feels you *must* give him what he asks and there is no other way. Let the person know there are other options, several of which that will probably be acceptable to him. Give him choices that allow him a way out of this threat without losing his dignity.

CHAPTER 8

Violence

The final stage of anger is violence. Most angry people do not become violent. It takes a huge leap to go from venting or intimidating to actually transgressing the external laws against assault and the internal restraints that inhibit it. I hope our previous discussion has provided insights and intervention skills to help defuse people's anger before it escalates into violence. Sometimes, however, listening might not be enough to calm a verbally abusive person; setting limits to someone's hostility may make her more belligerent, especially when someone's rage cannot be controlled and boils over into violence. Anger and aggression, abetted by anxiety, accelerate into assault. You are pushed, punched, slapped, kicked or, more harmfully, bludgeoned, stabbed or shot.

Whereas anger through the earlier stages was an expression of standing up for oneself and in more intense stages an expression of standing up to you, now anger is used to knock you down. Getting "in your face" is no longer to scare you but to be closer to you in order to hit you; shouting is not to be heard but to energize the person to attack you; threatening is done and now is the time for action. "Sticks and stones may break my bones but names will

never hurt me"; now name calling is over and you're about to have
your bones broken. A person's angry barking might once have been
worse than her bite, but it is her bite that is now about to hurt you.
The shouting match between the client and Gayle, who had to have
the last word, escalated from what began as an argument into a verbal altercation and finally into the client hitting the manager.
"That's what I think of your last word!"

The angry person's violence usually has a goal: to get what he
wants through physical force when nothing else—including threatening bodily attack—would procure it. Aggressively "being in your
face" or slamming his fist on the table were not sufficient warning
that you were next if you did not capitulate to his demands and so
now you get slammed in the face. Think of the stage-by-stage
examined man Bart who was angry at the Social Security clerk for
not giving him his benefit check. He originally yelled out of frustration, became hostile and when, after failing to get his money
even after threatening violence, he felt he "had it", he leaped from
his chair to strike Robin. It was a matter of hurt or be hurt and
Bart had had enough of her hurting him and so it was time for him
to hurt her.

Sometimes the violent person does not give a warning. We
have been examining a typical cycle of anger that builds from frustration to rage and concludes when the person reaches his "boiling
point" and replaces verbal abuse with physical abuse. But violence
does not have to be the culmination of mounting anger finally
exploding in physical force: a trajectory you can observe and hopefully intervene in while still in its more manageable incipient stages.
Violence can instead be the result of a controlled, calculated and
cold-blooded plan to hurt you. Maybe the person learned in childhood or sometime later in life that physical force is the best
means—and maybe the only means—to overcome obstacles that
stand in the way of one's goals. So without warning he hits you to
get what he wants. It is pragmatic. He wants something, you will
not give it and so he hits you to get it. You do not control him by
withholding; he controls you by hitting. An emergency room nurse

told me of a patient who brought in his wife who had a high fever and when told there was a long time to wait and to please have a seat, he did not yell or complain and instead suddenly grabbed the nurse and demanded his wife be seen immediately.

A person who hurts you for withholding what he needs often blames you for forcing him to hurt you. We earlier examined how blaming you for his adversity makes the person angry; now he hits you not only because he blames you for denying what he needs but also because you deserve to be hit. He is the victim—even though he hit you—because you could have given him the voucher, exchanged the defective item, maintained his employment or done whatever it was he expected you to do. But from his viewpoint you chose not to do it and therefore should be hurt, just as you hurt him.

Aggression is not merely standing up and knocking you down in order to get what the person wants but to punish you for hurting her. It is to even the score, to pay you back for what you did to her, to teach you a lesson for the hurt you caused. The violent act is not even necessarily a solution to a problem, because now the person inflicts harm regardless of whether the harm will procure what she wants. She hurts you even knowing she will not get what she wants, because it is simply out of revenge. "An eye for an eye, a tooth for a tooth." Or the person might be the earlier discussed sociopath who assaults you simply for the sadistic pleasure of seeing you in pain. More extreme, she can be the student who feels humiliated and so shoots her teacher and fellow students or the disgruntled worker who goes "postal" for being fired. More typically she is the social work client, the nurse/doctor's patient, the store clerk's customer, who hurts you for the hurt you supposedly caused her.

Return to the image of a motorist who is angry because you interfered with his driving. He no longer simply yells or gives you the finger and instead vengefully pursues you in order to drive you off the road. Remember also the scenario of a person you accidentally bumped. He expressed his anger in previous stages by cursing or threatening, but at this point he pushes you back to get even with you. Consider further the person who verbally abuses his partner but subsequently physically hurts her as punishment for whatever slight he feels she caused him. And do not forget the earlier mentioned competitive athlete who could not tolerate losing matches and who one time was so angry at his partner for presumably costing their victory that he forcefully hurled a ball at him.

None of these people got anything out of their violence except the satisfaction of hurting someone they blamed for hurting them. A secondary benefit they may receive is that their violent act makes them feel as though they regained some of the control they felt they momentarily lost when cut off the road or bumped or slighted. Their retribution undid or mitigated the hurt they experienced. Earlier I described Susie, whose anger at her husband's insensitivity was meant to emotionally push him away from making her feel vulnerable and subsequently became hostile when he insisted on confronting her anger: "Your yelling at me feels like your banging me on the head and then when I tell you about this you bang me even harder for my wanting to talk about it." Derrick's confronting Susie's anger felt like an assault on her vulnerability as well as on her ability to feel in control and one day, feeling she could no longer take his intrusiveness, she physically knocked him out of the way as she stormed out of the house. "There, now you really can say I've banged you on the head!"

Protect Yourself

You are about to be hit, kicked, stabbed or shot. Your listening skills and limit setting has had no effect on defusing the person's anger. She does not even care about "getting away with it", because all that matters is hurting you for having hurt her. The fact that she is going to do so is imminent and irreversible. De-escalation is no longer about defusing the person's anger, because the move toward hurting you has been set in motion and getting her to back down from it is not an option. Her goal is to hurt you; your goal is to protect yourself.

The enraged customer who "lost" her assigned window seat and was "in the face" of the airline representative did not have to move closer to him in order to strike him for infuriating her. He, however, should have seen the violence coming and been ready for it. He should have recognized desperation in the accelerating intensity of the customer's anger and in the deterioration of her logic and control that could easily explode in violence. Therefore he should have necessitated a plan for what to do should violence happen so that he would not have been hurt.

I have also referred to the situation of a motorist who became angry when cut off and then pursued the offending driver to force him to pull over; he then got out of his car, walked over to the other driver and, when that person rolled down the window to talk, punched him in the face. The victim in this scenario now knows he should have recognized in the man's fury and aggressive march toward his car the potential for physical assault. He thereby should have protected himself against that possibility by, for example, not rolling his window down in anticipation of the assault. However, he had much to learn about angry people and how to defuse them.

Try to Stay Calm
It is easy to freeze in fear and do something reckless when someone like an irate motorist frightens you. Remember the earlier discussion on the fight/flight response to feeling endangered. You can freeze out of fear or overreact by becoming violent yourself. Instead, the first step in protecting yourself when you are about to be hurt, as in responding to any angry person, is to try to stay calm. This is the first time I advise *try* rather than simply *stay calm*. I say *try*, because it is very challenging not to panic or overreact when you are about to be hurt. But this makes staying calm even more critical. We examined in each of the previous stages the importance of staying calm in order to de-escalate a person's anger, but now you need to stay calm in order to protect yourself from harm.

Remaining calm when confronted with unavoidable danger allows you to resist the urge to overreact and instead to assess the best way to protect yourself. The fight/flight response not only affects the production of more adrenaline to make you stronger but also induces more chemicals in your brain that produce a tunnel type of perception that helps you focus exclusively on the danger at hand. While being focused is beneficial, its downside is that it makes you only see what is immediately in front of you—the fist or knife—and thereby possibly makes you miss the bigger picture of what is available around you to help you escape being hurt.

For example, rather than foolishly be a hero and grab an assailant's gun or knife or rather than flee when you should fight, staying calm helps you assess the dangerous situation. An angry person approaches a situation as if to hurt you and so you want to stay calm and notice the look in his face. Does he have a weapon in his hands or are his hands in his pockets where there might be a hidden weapon? Are there objects in his vicinity he can use to hurt you? Is he bigger than you or pumped on drugs that cause him to be perniciously out of control? From this assessment you can ascertain what not to do (overreact) and what to do to defend yourself. The father of the earlier discussed heroin addict had previously experienced his daughter's rage when she was withdrawing from the drug and so should have not been surprised when one night at dinner she threw a table knife at him after he said he would not financially support her drug habit.

A tourist in San Francisco saw a man being assaulted and tried to stop it. He was fatally stabbed. A few months later I thought of this incident when I saw a man viciously yelling and pushing a woman. I was amazed no one was doing anything about it and I was not going to be one of those who ignored someone being assaulted. I was about to intervene when I remembered the stabbing situation in San Francisco. This prompted me to stop my instinctual reaction and to quickly assess what was the best and safest way to help the woman being attacked.

I am not judging the man who was stabbed trying to save the victim. I was not there and do not know what he was thinking or the other details of the situation, so I do not know whether he was heroic or foolish. But I do know you need to stay calm in these situations so as not to overreact and to be better able to assess how to intervene effectively. Thus in my situation of witnessing the woman be attacked, I reminded myself to stay calm and examine what was going on. I noticed the person was wearing a jacket, under which easily could be concealed a weapon such as a knife or a gun. He also was bigger than I, making a physical rescue dangerous. So instead of immediately trying to stop the assailant, I called 911 on my cell phone and moved close enough to shout to the man that the police were coming and he better get out of there. He yelled at the woman one more time—which helped him save face in front of me and her— and ran away. I may not have been the hero who physically jumped into the fray to save the day, but by staying calm and assessing the best way to intervene I was able to prevent the woman and myself from being hurt.

Avoiding a physical altercation is always preferable. If you can simply walk away from a physical altercation then do that. You might find yourself hesitating, wondering if you or others will think it cowardly. Resist this thought and simply get yourself out of danger. Make sure you remain aware of the assailant as you walk away, for you do not want him attacking you from behind. Also important is that when you need to flee danger, do your best not to leave others vulnerable.

Face Your Assailant

Let's return again to Tom, the client who did not get his medicine and whose anger toward the receptionist finally exploded in his reaching over the desk and grabbing her. Bonnie should have been prepared for this possibility—having observed the various warning signs in Tom's behavior described in the previous chapters—and so made note of what to do if he did try to hurt her. When he reached over the desk and tried to grab her, she should have been ready to back away from him and achieve a safe distance. If Tom then subsequently began to walk around the desk to more directly get at Bonnie, she could have quickly retreated into the office behind her, closed the door and called the police. There were no other people in the waiting area since it was the end of the day and so Bonnie needed to be aware that she had no one in the vicinity to help her (nor anyone who could be subject to his aggression in her place).

If you are not able to escape an assailant, as might be the case if you are in an office with no egress except the one blocked by the assailant, look for an object you can use to protect yourself or find a barrier to distance yourself from the attacker. Stand behind a desk or couch if available or hold a chair between you and the assailant. Do not hesitate to *yell* for help. It might secure someone's attention and might also cause the assailant to flee. The Social Security worker who could not give her client Bart his benefits check recognized in the man's mounting fury that he was about to lose control and possibly become violent and so was prepared for an attack when Bart suddenly leapt from his chair and reached out toward her. Robin quickly moved back from him, yelled for help and the angry client was subdued by security before he could hurt her.

When no help is forthcoming and no escape is available, physically protect yourself the best you can. Here are a few tips that might be helpful in defending yourself against an attack:

- If the person approaches to grab you and you cannot back away, keep your head lowered and duck down. More aggressively, try to bear-hug the person so as to pin his arms (like a boxer) until you can get help by yelling.
- If the person has you in his grasp, first explicitly and firmly tell him to let you go. Speak loudly so others might hear. If the assailant refuses to let go, try to escape by twisting out of the hold.
- If he has you by the throat, grab his arms and push up.
- If he is holding your hair do not try to pull away. You want to minimize injury to yourself. Instead, grab the hand holding your hair and then pull away.
- If he is about to punch you try to get out of his reach. Failing that, move your hand up to block the assault.
- If it is a kick, have your hands ready to block at the lower reaches.

Derrick, who continued to insist his wife Susie talk about her anger in spite of her hostile warning that he needed to stop pressuring her, should have been prepared when she tried to hit him. Rather than being struck, he should have been ready to move away from her blow or at least quickly raise his hands to physically block the blow.

Derrick, however, was surprised rather than prepared for his partner's physical attack. Should this happen to you, should you be hit, move with it. To "roll with the punch" sounds like a cliché but is real, because if you stiffen, you take the impact of the punch directly. You instead want to move with it so as to not be impacted as hard.

In the event of an attack, you, like so many others, will probably not think of any of these various techniques to defend yourself. Simply do whatever it takes to escape being hurt. (It is also helpful to have taken a self-defense class.)

Use Self-Defense

These defensive measures protect you from an assault, but they fall short of actually physically hitting the person to stop his hitting you. If doing whatever it takes to protect yourself means hurting the other person to get him to stop assaulting you, then that is what you must do. Ideally you do not want to hurt the person, preferring instead all the previously discussed means of escape, such as exiting or yelling for help. But that is the ideal and the reality is that you simply might have to become physically forceful to protect yourself. If you have to fight—and that is the only reason to fight: that you *have to*—then do so. Be prepared for when you hit the assailant that you will probably be hit back, even harder.

Remember, however, that doing whatever it takes to protect yourself has its limits. A usual legal definition of protecting yourself is one of reasonable force, which can be defined as using enough physical force to protect you. Anything more than that is no longer reasonable.

If you stop a physical assault, for example, and the person flees but you chase him and hit him, you are no longer defending yourself.

(You are also exposing yourself to being further hurt.) You are instead being retaliatory or punitive. The assault has probably pumped you with earlier discussed adrenaline-infused anger and you escalate the situation into an aggressive attack as opposed to defending yourself.

A person in San Francisco had his house burglarized while he was home and the intruder had a gun, which the homeowner was able to knock out of the burglar's hand and grab. The assailant was running out of the house when the homeowner shot him. The homeowner was arrested for assault even though he and his home had been victimized. The problem was that he was no longer protecting himself when the assailant was running. Instead he had become an assailant.

We need to remember that we act more aggressively in the elevated fight/flight state. This is good when we are protecting ourselves, but it can lead to the victim becoming the aggressor and vice versa. It is essential for you to remind yourself that physically fighting an assailant should go only as far as to protect yourself.

If you have been physically hurt in an assault, try to find a safe place until the assailant is gone. Then call the police or yell for help, but do not think the danger is necessarily over. The person could still come back to prevent you from calling the police, so be on your guard. When I was assaulted fifteen years ago trying to protect a social worker, as mentioned in the introduction, I immediately closed the door and locked it behind the assailant after he walked out of the office. This protected all of us in the office from his return. At the time, I wish I had the knowledge and skills presented in these pages whereby I would have recognized this person's potential for assaultive behavior and, if I was unable to de-escalate his anger, then at least I would have been prepared to defend myself against his violence. I instead was hit and even later experienced some delayed psychological reactions to being hit, which brings up the importance of post assault debriefing.

LEARN SELF-PROTECTION

Taking the time to prepare yourself now can make a big difference if you are ever physically attacked.

- What are some preventative measures you can take to protect yourself (e.g., taking a self-defense class, knowing your exits, having a code word/phrase with co-workers)?
- Understand the difference between self-defense and assault. Be sure to limit your physical interaction to only self-defense.
- Learn to identify anger warning signs and anticipate violence from people.
- Create exit strategies. If it helps you feel better prepared, imagine several different scenarios of facing angry people in your workplace, on the road, in the store, etc., and determine various ways to safely exit each location.
- Know the phone numbers for emergency response or program the numbers into your phone's speed dial.

CHAPTER 9

CHAPTER 9

Post Assault Debriefing

The anger and violence is over. You have been physically or verbally abused and now, after it is finished, what do you do? If you were physically hurt you need to go to the hospital. You might then think it is over. But it is not over until you have taken the time to understand both what happened to you and its emotional impact.

You may believe the crisis is over, but anyone who has been verbally or physically assaulted has been in some way adversely affected. You might feel victimized, angry at being mistreated or vulnerable, as if that which made you secure and in control has been taken away. You might feel resentful of those who did not help you, even spiteful toward those who judge or pity you. You could also feel guilty, as if the assault was your fault. If only you had been more understanding, more caring or done something differently. One of my employees was cruelly cursed by a client and afterward told me, "It really had to be my fault. He is much too nice of a person to say things like that without having in some way been provoked."

You might think the episode is done and you are fine, that you can handle being verbally abused or assaulted. I have seen this attitude in too many people who were attacked but who later exhibited any number of post-traumatic stress responses. It happened to me after I was assaulted. For several years thereafter I felt a queasiness in my stomach any time someone became threatening or "got in my face." The previously discussed manager Gayle—who was involved in the increasingly hostile shouting match until finally the client struck her—was so understandably shaken by the altercation that afterward she took disability time off from work.

Post-traumatic stress can happen to you after you are threatened or attacked. You may find yourself obsessed with the incident, ruminating on it, asking "why me" and maybe even plotting revenge. You could become less confident, besieged with doubts and self-medicating through drinking/drugs. Nightmares, flashbacks to the experience and a general sense of helplessness, depression, restlessness and even suicidal thoughts are common symptoms in people after an assault. You may distance yourself from others, avoid conflict and feel defensive or paranoid. Do not be surprised if you experience somatic symptoms such as headaches, fatigue, or insomnia.

Talking with someone after a verbal or physical assault is the best way to manage what happened to you and to understand your feelings about it. If you are an executive at a large company, the human resource person could aid you. If you are a professional, talk to a colleague. If the situation occurred at work and you have a supervisor, meeting with this person is essential. If the assault took place outside of work or you would feel more comfortable, talk with friends or family and maybe seek professional counseling. Talking to someone shortly after the incident is critical to help you feel safe as well as to slow the anxiety and adrenaline pumping in your body.

Perhaps you are not ready to immediately talk about how you feel, but you should be open to it at a later time. It is common to have delayed reactions to an abusive or violent encounter. Joyce, a woman who was the victim of her partner's vicious verbal abuse and who fortunately was able to get the professional help for both of them to successfully learn to communicate without the verbal violence, came to me years later to talk about how good the relationship had become but also how she still periodically physically flinched or emotionally recoiled when her partner innocuously said something that, while not overtly aggressive, reminded her of the days when she was the victim of his violence.

Whether immediately or some time after a verbally/physically abusive situation, talking with another person will help you make sense of what happened and feel more in control. You will realize that it was not your fault and that you are not responsible for others' actions. Even if you made a mistake that contributed to the incident, talking about it will help you understand your response and learn better ways of dealing with such issues. Remember the earlier discussed Derrick whose insensitivity angered his wife. In the end, Susie struck Derrick when he continued to press her to process her feelings in spite of her very clear warning that she was going to hurt him if he did not stop pressuring her. She ceased coming to counseling after that violent incident, but he and I talked about his responsibility in the altercation, how he felt about what happened and what he could learn from it.

Whatever precipitates your being the victim of someone's verbal or violent abuse, talking about it will help you realize that, even with the best application of the de-escalation skills we discussed earlier, sometimes listening will defuse a person's anger while other times it will not diminish it or that clearly setting limits will help one person restrain his aggressive impulse while it may have the opposite effect on another person. Remind yourself to remain calm when you are responding to an angry or hostile person and know you have done your best to defuse the situation and protect yourself from harm.

ASSESS YOUR ENCOUNTER
WITH AN ANGRY PERSON

Recall an encounter with an angry person and reflect on these questions:

- What stage of anger did the person express? Did he escalate through stages?
- What did you do to try to defuse the person's anger? Did it work?
- What would you have done differently?
- What things were out of your control?

Seek a trusted family member, friend, clergy person or supervisor and discuss the situation with him or her. Ask for his or her insight. If you feel you need further counseling, ask for professional recommendations and meet with a counselor.

CONCLUSION

I mentioned earlier in this book that fifteen years ago I had an incident with a hostile client. At that time I had not developed the insights into angry people that would have helped me recognize the potential for violence in this person nor the practical techniques with which to defuse his anger before it became violent. I had successfully managed other people's anger and was confident I would similarly de-escalate his. I was not prepared when my intervention did not calm his hostility. It instead made him angrier; so angry that he hit me.

We all encounter angry people: an irate co-worker, a difficult customer, a partner in domestic abuse, a drug addict, a bully, an enraged driver, a volatile friend. If we cannot always defuse these people's anger then at least we should know how *not* to escalate it into violence. I failed at the latter with my client. I mistook his anger for an expression of frustration, which, as described, is the earliest stage of anger and probably the most common form. I intervened with my client using techniques that would have been appropriate for someone who felt ignored and whose yelling was a way to be heard but which for my client escalated, rather than de-escalated, his anger.

Listening and empathy did not calm my client as they would have the earlier described client Tom, who was not able to get his medication, because he was late for his doctor appointment. He was frustrated that the receptionist did not listen to how important the medicine was for him. Many of us periodically encounter similar types of frustrating situations: it might be a rude clerk, an insensitive boss, a child who does not listen or an annoying acquaintance. We do not go ballistic or become violent, but, like Tom, we do sometimes become angry. We vent our frustrations, demand respect and sometime raise our voices to be heard. Our anger is a healthy way of standing up for ourselves and of not accepting being ignored or victimized.

At times, all of us become frustrated or angry and we usually know what it takes to calm it: someone listens to your frustration and you no longer feel ignored; the store clerk apologizes for being inattentive and you feel better; your boss says he understands what you are saying and you no longer feel disrespected. These and other responses examined in earlier chapters have a calming effect on angry people. Listening to what frustrates them—rather than trying to get them to stop yelling—helps irate people feel heard. Those who yell in order to be heard will stop yelling when they are heard.

The client who struck me, however, did not care if I listened to him. His anger was not an expression of standing up for himself as I thought it to be and instead was a way of standing up in order to knock me down. He knocked me down, because my misreading of his anger made him angrier. He probably felt like I was diminishing the gravity of his situation. My client was not a person who was frustrated and who simply needed to be heard, nor was he defensively angry, which is the next stage of anger. The defensively irate person, remember, is someone who becomes angry not only because he is ignored but also because being ignored makes him feel belittled or emotionally hurt. He never learned to directly manage these feelings and instead finds it preferable to yell about being ignored than to feel humiliated or like a failure from it. In his viewpoint, it is better to be mad than sad.

Think of Bart, the man who was angry at Social Security for denying his benefits. Robin's listening to this man was not sufficient to placate his anger, because it only acknowledged the anger he felt about being denied a check while leaving unaddressed a deeper and more intense anger about how the experience humiliated him. His yelling at Robin was an emotional wall behind which were kept hidden hurt feelings. To protect these feelings, Bart expressed an aggressive standing up to those who made him feel vulnerable. Defusing his anger was not as easily accomplished as simply listening to what angered him, because his anger also protected him against being emotionally hurt. Instead Bart needed to know not only that he was heard for what angered him but also that he was validated in how it made him feel. Then he would have had less reason to be defensively angry.

The client who struck me did not care if I validated his feelings. In fact, it made him angrier to think that I thought I could calm him by saying I understood how he felt. This might have been because he was being difficult. The difficult person intentionally irritates you and is uncooperative or argumentative so as to drag you into a contest of wills to prove to you she is smarter or better than you. Your task is to avoid this contest; to not let her drag you into her drama. You need to listen to her anger and support how she feels but at the same time make it clear you will not become entangled in her need to compete with or annoy you. As a result she will back away from being compelled to test your limits or irritate you. It is hard to be difficult with someone who works with you rather than against you.

Remember the examination of Andy, the man who was uncooperative with his wife Claire even over small matters as a way to be difficult and demonstrate who was in control. Do not confuse Andy's difficult ways, as I almost did, with Ryan's, who created difficult situations in order to get angry about them, thereby having a reason to criticize his partner and storm out of the house so as to avoid doing something with his partner that he did not want to do. His anger was not a contest of wills and instead was a hostile attempt to bully his partner. De-escalating this belligerence cannot be accomplished with listening skills or validation. Hostility makes the person feel in control of both herself *and* you and she will not readily relinquish her anger because that would mean letting go of control. De-escalation begins with recognizing the intensity of the person's hostility: an aggressive body posture, a vicious stare, meanness, bullying. This person does not yell, as she did in earlier stages, *about* what angered her and instead viciously yells *at* the one who upset her. It is also an anger that no longer is an expression of standing up for oneself in order to get you to listen and instead is used to "get in your face" in order to *make* you listen.

I did not look for these signs in the hostile client who struck me and so did not recognize the extent of his anger. As a result I did not intervene appropriately. Had I recognized the signs and had Ryan's partner recognized them in Ryan's belligerence, we would have then tried to de-escalate their hostility by acknowledging the intensity of their anger so as to not make them feel we were challenging their control. At the same time we would have firmly let them know that we were not intimidated by their anger and thereby we also were in control. This means letting an angry person know you understand his anger but that he has to rein it in. "I get your message loud and clear, but getting in my face will not work with me."

A firm, albeit understanding, approach can help defuse some people's hostility, but it can make others explode in rage when they feel the anger that maintains their control is being challenged. Anger is not the problem with rage: uncontrollable anger is the problem. Rage is not merely an extreme expression of a person's anger but of anger the person cannot manage. Ranting is not simply venting and instead is feelings bursting forth that the person cannot contain or that are slipping out of her grasp.

Think back to Emily, the woman who became hysterically angry when another driver took her parking place. I could not calm her with a rational suggestion that we would find another place to park nor with an expectation that she needed to stop ranting. When she screamed, "I can't take people doing this to me anymore," it was obvious she needed help to prevent her rage from spinning out of control. So I calmly got her to focus her attention on my effort to bring her feelings under control. "Emily, look at me. I know it feels crazy right now, but I promise we are going to get this situation under control."

Telling the enraged person she can regain control makes her feel a little safer with her overwhelming feelings, but it does not do so without your setting strict limits to her rage. Your approach should be not simply, "It's going to be okay" but rather that it is going to be okay and that those unbridled feelings can—and need to be—controlled. "Emily, look at me. This is an entirely manageable situation and so I need you to get a hold of yourself."

Some people become enraged when their anger is out of control while others control their feelings by doubling their aggressive efforts to control you, which is what my client did when he suddenly hit me. However, some people give a warning that they are going to hit you. They threaten to hurt you if you do not acquiesce to their demands. Whereas earlier stage anger expressed a person's standing up for himself or even standing up to you to push you around verbally, now it is standing up to threaten to push you around *physically*. The person has done all he can to make you comply and believes he has no other way except that of threatening harm. Tom, as discussed, originally expressed his frustration toward the receptionist for not giving him his medicine and in the end, when she did not comply, he threatened to hurt her. Bart said he would not leave the social worker's office without his Social Security check and if it meant someone was going to get hurt then that is what it would take.

You might be tempted to respond aggressively to these people's threats, but this does not usually defuse the threats and instead makes people feel pushed into a corner where rather than "lose face" they act on their threats. This does not mean you ignore a threat or comply with it—thereby making you appear weak or frightened. Instead, let the person know you understand the seriousness of his threat while at the same time telling him you will not tolerate it: "I can see you're angry, but it's not okay to threaten me. So stop the threats and let's see what we can do."

I heard Amy, a social worker, use almost these exact words in responding to a threatening client who then warned her of what would happen if she did not produce what he wanted. "I've had enough of your stalling and now you leave me no choice!" Let the threatening person know he does have other choices besides acting on his threat. Give him an "out" that makes him see he is not stuck in a corner where the only way to "save face" is to be violent. If that does not work, your last recourse is to warn him of the consequences for his threats. But know that warning a person about repercussions can make him feel he has no choice but to act on his threat before you act on yours. So stating repercussions should be done in a way that minimizes this likelihood. Get the person to *think* about consequences. There are social prohibitions against violence and something has stopped the threatening person from thinking about them, which you want him to reconsider so as to understand how repercussions for his actions will outweigh the benefits he derives from them. "I know what you said but think what would happen if you did it."

You have done all you can to defuse a person's threat or to help control his rage and in the end he physically hurts you to get what he wants. Or maybe he hurts you not to get what he wants but to get back at you, to even the score, for denying him what he wanted. That is what happened with my client who hit me, because I interfered in his verbal attack on the social worker. Most angry people, unlike this client, do not become violent. It takes a huge leap to go from venting or intimidating to actually transgressing the laws against assault and the internal restraints that inhibit it. Sometimes, however, listening or setting firm limits does not defuse a person's frustration or control her rage. Anger and aggression accelerate into assault. Before, they energized a person to stand up for himself and even to stand up to you, but now they make him stand up to knock you down. This can happen as when my client stood up from his chair and suddenly struck me. Less literally, it means in the end people like Tom hit the receptionist who would not give him his medication, Susie slapped her husband Derrick for not taking her threats seriously, Emily rammed her car into the other driver's car for taking her parking spot and so on.

Whether out of retaliation or to get what he wants, while facing an angry person you may be about to get hurt. Angry name calling may not hurt you but "sticks and stones may break your bones" and your bones may be about to be broken. Violence might be imminent and irreversible. De-escalation therefore is no longer about defusing the person's anger and instead is about protecting you. I should have seen the signs of potential violence in my client and if I could not have defused his hostility through the various techniques described in these pages then I should have been prepared for the violence that was to come. Bonnie should have recognized in Tom's escalating anger the potential for physical abuse and known what to do to protect herself from it. Derrick should have taken his wife's threats seriously and when he did not, he should have been prepared to prevent what happened next.

Fifteen years ago I knew neither what to do to protect myself from being hurt by an angry client nor how to effectively defuse his belligerence and prevent it from escalating into violence. Since that time I have worked with hostile and enraged people, with families whose verbal abuse cycled into physical abuse, with friends who are volatile and bosses who are bullies, with drug addicts and people whose mental health issues induced intense anger and sometimes violence. I have learned how to listen to their frustrations, validate their defensive anger, help them gain control over their rage, rein in their hostility and, finally, when at times unable to prevent a threat of physical abuse from becoming acted on, to protect myself from harm. I have presented in this book the resulting insights into people's anger and hostility as well as the techniques to de-escalate them. I hope that through this information and your reflection on it you have gained better knowledge of how to defuse people's anger and to protect yourself from harm.

NOTES